ARCHITECTS OF CHANGE:

Practical tools for executives to build, lead, and sustain organizational initiatives.

Dr. Jim Bohn

PYRAMIDS, TEMPLES, SKYSCRAPERS, CATHEDRALS, AND CASTLES ALL HAVE ONE THING IN COMMON: THEY HAD AN ARCHITECT. SOMEONE WITH A VISION FOR A STRUCTURE. SOMEONE WHO DESIGNED THE STRUCTURE AND MANAGED THE LABOR FOR THE STRUCTURE, WORKING DILIGENTLY TO SEE THE STRUCTURE COMPLETED. EVERY NEW CORPORATE INITIATIVE IS A NEW CONCEPT WAITING TO BECOME REALITY, REQUIRING A LEADER WHO IS AN ARCHITECT OF CHANGE.

THAT'S YOU.

ENDORSEMENTS

"As a master architect of Change Management, Dr. Bohn has provided a clear, actionable process for those responsible for guiding change in any organizational setting."

Jonathan E. Dehlinger, Ph.D.

"Rooted in profound simplicity and clearly based on 'ground level' experience; in a business world where the only thing constant is change, this is an easy read loaded with actionable insights and tools that help de-risk organizational changes, large and small."

Agostino Renna, President & CEO, GE Lighting, EMEA

"Using examples that we all can relate to, Jim has once again simplified a complex topic into a usable playbook for getting things done. With tips and hints for creating change that sticks, this latest work from Jim is now a welcome part of my leadership toolkit."

James Mylett, Senior Vice-President, Comfort Systems USA

"In the book, *Architects of Change: Practical Tools for Executives to Build, Lead and Finish Organizational Initiatives,* Jim has done the research for everyone involved in change management, and put it into an applicable toolkit for utilization."

Steve Meyers, Director, Central US • Field Service, Vivint

"Dr. Bohn's book provides a very practical assessment of what it really takes to lead successful change within an organization for those in executive roles – highly recommended for senior leaders."

Kerry J. Brunner Vice-President, Total Rewards, Ministry Health Care

"A must read for Company Execs who are leading and/or involved in change initiatives. This book provides the needed tools to influence change and keep your company out of the 'valley of despair.'"

Dave Hamilton, Regional Vice President, Regis Corporation

"It's not enough to create the burning platform for change—leaders have to create a culture that's ready for change. Jim Bohn provides a very practical approach to fostering the kind of culture that embraces new ways of doing things."

Charles Hughes, Director, Field Service, Walgreen Co.

DEDICATION

There are several people in my life who framed my thinking and continue to influence my work ethic. My brother, Richard Gall, is an autodidact; a self-taught man who developed significant engineering skills simply out of his own cognitive resources. He is very smart and his aptitude for fixing things is second to none.

The second person is my brother, Scott, who is a mechanical genius and who can fix any car, anytime, under any conditions.

The third person is my son, Joseph James Bohn, who persisted to become a Journeyman Tool and Die Maker. They are all common-sense, down-to-earth people who simply know how to get the job done. I never quite achieved the bar they raised, and I had to settle for a Ph.D. to compensate. *I'm not kidding.*

They are part of a greater pedigree that came from my father, James Leo Bohn. He was a soldier, a welder, an orphan and a mechanic. He could not write his name. Yet his ethic of 'get the job done' has stuck with me throughout these past decades. He clearly influenced the way I think and the way I work. It is to him who I owe the most for my success in life and, to him, I dedicate this book.

J.B.

Table of Contents

ACKNOWLEDGEMENTS

No one writes a book without significant inspiration from others, both as to the content, and to the actual work of writing. The work of writing is simply too hard to go it alone; one needs the inspiration of others to complete the work. One also needs good critics, who are truly interested in the author's success; critics who will provide guidance and useful commentary that will improve the overall product.

So, I am grateful for intellects like Don Kirkey, Jeff Walters and Tom Lowery, who have pushed me very hard through the years, setting expectations for levels of excellence well beyond what I would have attempted without their coaching. I am grateful to Agostino Renna, Jon Dehlinger and James Mylett for their insights and willingness to support me along the way. Mr. Renna is a powerhouse leader with immense ability to inspire. Dr. Dehlinger made a significant impression on me long ago, which inspired me to persist in attaining the doctorate. James Mylett is a true philosopher of leadership, whose achievements have spurred me on to greater efforts. These men are all extremely gifted leaders who have inspired me by their own major and significant achievements. Among these brilliant and capable "A" students, I am a "C" student at best.

I also wish to thank Jon Heaton, Dave Hamilton, Charles Hughes, Kerry Brunner, Steve Myers and Charles Johnson for taking the time to read and comment on the manuscript as it was being developed. They have all been very helpful in their thoughts and suggestions.

Finally, no book can be completed without a good editor. I'd like to thank my wife, Mary Jo, for her time spent in the preliminary editing, and Mary Boyle at Seven Hills Creations for her editorial and technical expertise that truly brought the book to life.

FOREWORD

Every organization these days—whether corporate, military, government, academic, nonprofit, or religious—is in the midst of significant change; it has become the constant in our world. As a result, as Dr. Jim Bohn tells us, all management has become Change Management.

The bookstore shelves groan with Change Management books because of this phenomena of continual change. This practical little book is different from many of the others—it is about change leadership. This book will help prepare you to assume the critical role of Architect of Change. *The Architect of Change* is more than the passive role of executive sponsor. This book will help you be a better sponsor of change, but it will also guide you so that you know what to expect—and inspect—as you lead your organization through transformation.

As you will learn, details are critical for the success of change initiatives. Dr. Bohn will help you identify the right balance between strategic overview and detailed management, the "nuts and bolts" of Change Management.

You will face the barriers to change that exist in every organization, at the individual, managerial, and organizational levels. Ultimately, levering Dr. Bohn's wisdom—grounded in many years of hard-won insight from leading change in the corporate world—will help you build the change you are making into the DNA of the organization.

Don Kirkey, Ed.D.
Director, Leadership Development
Lowe's Companies, Inc.

EXECUTIVE SUMMARY

Executives and leaders develop organizational strategy that leads to major change. While leaders are often competent in sales, finance and marketing, Change Management skills learned in MBA courses are often forgotten when executives launch new organizational initiatives. And yet, Change Management skills are *critical* for effective implementation of new programs.

There is a need for executives to master and use specific change skills to ensure an ROI in both financial and human terms. That's what this book is all about. **This is the heart of change sponsorship** – the effort of leadership one must take to make the change part of organizational DNA. This is not a book about change tools or techniques – it is a call to leaders to use their leadership to ensure their organization achieves what it sets out to do. The Architect is someone who designs, builds, and leads a structure to completion. The same concepts are true in managing change. There is no time where Architects take their eye off the project, even though many others are doing the work.

To ensure the change is complete, leaders must be engaged at every step, as follows:

1. **Architects are involved with the Foundation** of change rationale, ensuring due diligence without procrastination, deliberately planning for executive leadership communications, and carefully defining metrics to ensure the change did what it was intended to do.

2. **Architects are involved with Launching the Change,** by ensuring the best team is in place, knowing the difference between a change leader and a project manager; preparing for consistent, intentional and regular communications; and, ensuring there is a feedback loop to prevent a change from going off course.

3. **Architects provide Day-to-Day Support of the Change** to ensure the change takes hold in the organization, including a clear understanding of the conflicts and resistance that may take place, and the 'changes within a change' that occur when a project is launched.

4. Most importantly, Architects learn the critical need to stay with the change until the capstone is put in place, **ensuring the change is Finished.**

Architects also provides a clear understanding of the many personae leaders must take on to manage the change, including Organizational Psychologist and Organizational Diplomat. The book also provides five critical principles for helping people adjust to change, including reduction of anxiety, breaking down training into distributed practice, and building trust.

Ultimately, executives need a plan to become effective Architects of Change. This book is not theory. It provides a blueprint built from extensive experience and research, and it will help you get the job done.

THE PRACTICAL TOOLS – ARCHITECT'S BLUEPRINT

FINISHING THE CHANGE
The Nuts and Bolts of Change

SUPERSTRUCTURE LAUNCHING THE CHANGE

1. Selection of Team Leadership
2. Team Selection
3. Develop an Intentional Communication Plan
4. Detailed Project Plan
5. Team Cadence
6. Feedback Loop to Assure Communication
7. System Issues - Details for IT changes

ARCHITECT BEHAVIORS

Managing Organizational, Managerial and Individual Barriers to Completion

1. Persistence
2. Clarity
3. Recognition
4. Managerial Check-in
5. Communicating to the End
6. Renewing Team Vigor

DAY-TO-DAY SUPPORT (WHAT TO EXPECT DURING CHANGE)

1. Knowing that there are "changes within a change".
2. Understanding and Managing Change Resistance
3. Managing Team Drama

FOUNDATION PREPARING FOR THE CHANGE

1. Developing the Rationale
2. Conducting Due Diligence
3. Deliberately Planning Effective Communication
4. Defining Initial Metrics

GROUNDWORK

There's a lot going on during a major organizational initiative.

ORGANIZATIONAL CRISIS:

"SOMETHING NEEDS TO CHANGE"

Dr. Miriam Alexander, president of Catalyst Industries, looked deeply concerned as she stared out her office window. William Tenwirth, her CFO, and Jonathan Smith, her COO, were sitting across from her. They heard a knock at the door.

"Good morning Dr. Alexander," a voice sounded from outside her door. It was Tina Vasquez, Global VP of Sales.

"Hello Tina, I'm glad you're here," Dr. Alexander responded. "Thanks for coming on such short notice. I saw the latest monthly reports. Is it accurate that we're down 12% business year-over-year? What's the source of this issue? Why are we losing business to our competitors?"

Tina nodded, "Our competition argues that CATALYST has no true centralized systems for technical support. That fact has caused sales losses in several major competitive situations. When global customers ask us whether we can take calls and support anywhere, the ultimate answer is 'no.'"

Dr. Alexander was a medical expert, not an operations specialist. "Well, what can be done? Clearly we're not the only organization in the world that has faced this issue."

Jonathan Smith, VP Operations, made a recommendation. "We could install a centralized system for global support. There are many tools available today. Corporations do this all the time—we simply grew too fast with our acquisitions."

Dr. Alexander turned to her CFO, William Tenwirth: "William, we have funds in capital planning for this year."

"Yes," he answered abruptly, "and I agree we need a system. In fact, my old company, Brewster, had an excellent system for tracking, support and parts ordering. I'm not sure why *you've* never invested in a global system, but I need to remind you that those funds are for R&D and facility maintenance."

Dr. Alexander responded, "Jonathan, let's get this started. You have the lead for now, but I want to meet together in one week."

As she adjourned the meeting, Dr. Alexander asked Tina Vasquez, "Do you think this will solve the problem we're facing?"

Tina responded, "I think it will make a major difference. I will inform my sales team today."

"Then let's make this change happen. Jonathan, you have the lead. Give me monthly reports."

* * * * * * * * * * *

Three months later ...

The organization struggled with the change; it failed, and they returned to their old, antiquated systems. What's more, they had invested $5,000,000 dollars and expended significant employee effort in the process. They had wasted their opportunity to make a change, they de-motivated their employees, and they lost organizational momentum.

This is not an uncommon outcome. How could it have been avoided?

Throughout this book, I provide snippets of real world challenges in managing change.

Real World Challenges:

THE PAIN OF CHANGE DURING ACQUISTIONS
Conversations with top Operations Executives

The elements of change in a merger and acquisition are complex and manifold. Several Vice-Presidents and leaders of businesses in the Southeastern Wisconsin area took an in-depth look at the challenges of merging two radically different cultures from the perspectives of both the acquiring and the acquired organizations.

The intention and design of the buying organization provide some of the first clues to understanding how well the integration will go. If the goal is to remove a competitor, versus gaining a company to acquire new skills and products, the approach is likely to be very different. One will provide growth opportunities, while another will invariably involve downsizing.

Several common issues presented themselves as key areas requiring communication during major integrations, including loss of key people, integration of health plans, and delivery of new 401 (k) plans and the commensurate loss of old ones. The challenges of redundancy in operations and staffing were also noted as key areas of communication. Clearly these issues have a strong impact on the acquired organization. These open issues mean a slowdown in employee energy; a taking of the foot off of the accelerator, which will ultimately end in loss of revenue. Delayed decision making on the part of the acquiring company can result in further loss.

To effectively manage change in these situations without serious loss of profit or human energy, executives need a toolkit of skills.

"Change is the law of life. Those who look only to the past or present are certain to miss the future."

John F. Kennedy

CHAPTER 1

SOME GROUNDWORK

FINISHING THE CHANGE
The Nuts and Bolts of Change

SUPERSTRUCTURE	DAY-TO-DAY SUPPORT
LAUNCHING THE CHANGE	(WHAT TO EXPECT DURING
1. Selection of Team Leadership	CHANGE)
2. Team Selection	1. Knowing that there are
3. Develop an Intentional	"changes within a change".
Communication Plan	2. Understanding and Managing
4. Detailed Project Plan	Change Resistance
5. Team Cadence	3. Managing Team Drama
6. Feedback Loop to Assure	
Communication	
7. System Issues - Details for	
IT changes	

FOUNDATION PREPARING FOR THE CHANGE
1. Developing the Rationale
2. Conducting Due Diligence
3. Deliberately Planning Effective Communication
4. Defining Initial Metrics

GROUNDWORK
There's a lot going on during a major organizational initiative.

If you're going to be held accountable for the effectiveness of a major organizational initiative and you need some practical tools, you need to read this book.

As a leader, you *know* change is the given, and you want to do it right. Here is a fast read, how-to manual to help you effectively finish the initiatives you undertake in your organization.

1. *Read this book to discover gaps in your knowledge as you begin a change.*

2. *Read this book to discover the weaknesses your organization will face during change.*

3. *Read this book with your executive team to build their skills.*

4. *Read this book to help you anticipate and address employee resistance to change.*

5. *Read this book to help your company more quickly reduce the organizational stress caused by change.*

6. *Read this book to raise questions with your change management team.*

You've heard the statistic that 70% of organizational changes fail. As an executive, you don't want to waste precious organizational resources when introducing a change, but you still may wonder, *"**What exactly is my role in leading a change, and where can I best apply my skills and influence to ensure our desired outcome?**"*

A few assumptions on my part:

- *You and your leadership team have already agreed to make this change.*

- *You and your leadership team are aligned on the scope of the change.*

- *You have budgeted some funds for a preliminary due diligence effort.*

- *The initiative is of major importance to your organization.*

- *You are personally committed to the success of the change.*

You're good at what you do.

You're good at many things. You've reached the top level of an organization because of your skill, knowledge, courage and political will, but organizational change requires those skills, and more. As an Architect, you want to ensure the dollars you spend on a change provides you with an expected return on investment. To accomplish that goal, you need a straightforward and effective way to understand how to use your skills to effectively manage change.

There are very specific things you need to do to increase the likelihood that your organizational change efforts and costs (financial, human and opportunity) pay off for your company.

There's a lot going on during a major organizational initiative.

Whatever your goal, here are some of the changes your initiative could likely induce in your organization. It looks like a lot of detail, because it is. *You need to know this will happen to your organization.*

The Impact of Organizational Initiatives

Behavior Changes – How will people be expected to act differently?
Business Rule Changes – How will we manage the business differently?
Compensation Plan Alignment – How will employees be compensated differently?
Conceptual Changes (the way employees see the world)
Culture Changes (Communication, Structure, Job Roles, Leadership Training)
Information Technology Systems
Leadership Changes – How will you transition your current leadership?
Mergers & Acquisitions
Policy Changes – Legal, HR, Finance, Operations
Process Changes
Product Releases
Relocations
Reorganization of staff and leadership
Reporting and measurement changes
Skill Changes – What new tools will people learn?
Technical Changes, including new data storage facilities
Terminology Changes
Workforce Management Soft Ware

Figure 1 – The impact of change on your organization

Yet even being good at what you do is not enough to ensure success

When it comes to managing change, your executive strengths can also be weaknesses. There is a risk that your skills can become liabilities. Your knowledge of Operations, Finance, Business Law, Sourcing, and Sales may actually prevent you from seeing the need for your *specific* strategic involvement in managing change. Your success in one area may blind you to what is necessary to effectively manage change. You may assert that change is as simple as "Just do it" but, deep down, you know it's not that easy. On a deeper level, you *know* how poorly things can go, because you've watched the failed initiatives of your former bosses and leaders, and you know the legends of their fall.

Your Executive Mindset drives your current approach to change

- **Get the job done.**

- **Don't waste my time with jargon**

- **Show me why I should set aside budget for Change Management**

But that may not be enough to ensure the successful implementation of a change.

You intuitively know that effective Change Management allows for smoother transitions, reducing corporate waste and protecting precious employee energy. Most importantly, effective Change Management ensures you got your money's worth.

You're good at what you do—I'm good at what I do

The material in this book is not theoretical. It was forged in the fires of real change projects in multiple organizations, and reviewed by leaders with extensive change experience in their own organizations.

With over 25 years of experience in a wide range of projects, ranging from M&A to standardizing uniforms for over 5,000 people, I have 'been there.' I have observed that when executives initiate large scale projects/strategies, they often do not have a clear sense of what *they* need to do to make the project successful. As the Blue Collar Scholar, my purpose is to make you successful.

So, what exactly is "Change Management?"

Change Management, as I define it, is simply this: the skill of helping people and organizations effectively adjust to new things.

You're skeptical, but interested in the concept of Change Management

You've heard the term "Change Management," but you're skeptical. You know Change Management 'gurus' don't know a whole lot about your business, and it shows when they make a presentation. You get a sense of "*KumBayah*" and you're not comfortable with spending money on 'fluff.' You may have trusted Change Management systems and invested heavily in CM models in the past, only to see your investments become a sunk cost (sometimes with a commensurate loss of business).

There are legitimate reasons for your skepticism

1.   You've heard presentations and invested in Change Management methodology, only to realize the change team was weak and ineffective. Some executives see CM as an ad hoc organization off to the side, brought in only as a last resort.

2.   Perhaps you've used trusted external resources (aka *Consultants*) to learn about a Change Management model, only to watch the changeover from the external resource result in a lack of continuity costing tens of thousands - or millions - of dollars. Your skepticism of Change Management is merited and, yet, you have had to manage change.

3. Sometimes you've done change the hard way, with brute force, or sometimes with organizational savvy, power

and effective political alliances. Sometimes you've done it because you were—drum roll—great Change Managers (though you didn't even have the title!)! There's a big need for you to understand your role in leading change.

Think about it this way:

All Management is Change Management

The simplest analogy I propose for Change Management is the pain and stress of relocation: the disruptions, the tension, and the stress are obvious as we shift from one location to another. This is the most commonly experienced form of change, but there's an even clearer way to explain Change Management to executives: all management is (ultimately) change management:

- Managers are responsible for inducing a form of change or their employment could be jeopardized (Corporations generally don't pay you to maintain the status quo - you're there to make something better).

- Most managers actually do make change happen, and many do it well. They show year-over-year improvement, and they are compensated for those successes.

- Managers, educators, and leaders know when "something's gotta change around here!" They see it, feel it in their gut, sense it, and know it.

CHANGE TIP

10 Basic Questions to Ask Before Starting Any Change

1. Why do you want to change?

2. What is the change?

3. Who is involved?

4. Who leads the change?

5. Who needs to know?

6. Where are the philosopher-kings and queens— the true organizational influencers?

7. Who will support those affected by the change?

8. What is the organizational impact?

9. Where are the risks?

10. Who is in charge of the details?

- Change has been a constant in business forever because businesses change to survive.

- Adjusting to the organizational changes imposed by new products takes major effort.

- In short, change is going on all the time.

Good Change Managers *do* have a specialized skill-set – they're good at what *they* do.

Change Management specialists have the psychological background and tools to help you achieve a smooth transition in your organizations. CMs have studied Individual Motivation, Group Dynamics, Leadership Influence, and Organizational Psychology – the real levers behind successful change.

Change management is still a bit 'ethereal' to me: Why the mystique?

Change Managers use multiple change models. While that's good, it sometimes confuses the users of the process. The Change Management Industry has developed a mind-boggling array of toolkits, frameworks, templates, job aids and other paraphernalia. No end-user can keep track of the stuff, but they do have binders of materials from various change workshops collecting dust on their bookshelves.

What can executives learn from the best CMs? This book is your opportunity to learn from my Change Management expertise, focusing exclusively on the executive role.

"There is nothing permanent, except change."

Heraclitus—Pre-Socratic Greek Philosopher

CHAPTER 2
HOW CHANGE AFFECTS YOUR ORGANIZATION

Real World Challenges:

THE IMPACT TO TEAMS DURING A MAJOR PROCESS CHANGE

The introduction of a new way to manage Service Operations, which included new technology, seemed simple until we began discovering the many groups that would be impacted by the change. At first, it seemed only 'local' groups would be affected, including service technicians and their management. As we began to move deeper into the project, it became obvious that many more groups were going to be affected by the change. Eventually, we had monthly meetings with over 35 organizational teams, ranging from finance to facilities management, to ensure they had a clear awareness of what to expect when the change was rolled out, and also to ensure they were engaged in what they needed to do to achieve change success. By engaging these teams, we had a successful roll-out.

Change impacts your *entire* organization, so let's step back and take a high-level look at organizational strata to examine how they will be affected by the change.

Affected Group	Impact
Executive Decisions - Organizational Level	Where change begins
Departments and Customers	Groups of people who are peripherally or closely connected to the change
Team Level	Teams within your organization
Mid-level Leaders	The critical group who leads the change
Individual Level	The 'led;' the people on the ground floor

Figure 2— How change impacts groups differently

I. Executive Decisions at the Organizational Level – Where change begins

Your new strategy is forcing a change. Your organization either (a) needs new technology, or (b) is reacting to a serious competitive threat, or (c) is seeking to outwit the competition, or (d) seeking organizational efficiencies.

A note of caution: Psychologists (Transtheoretical Model of Change - *Prochaska, DiClemente, and Norcross*) developed a program for individual change that tells us people spend a lot of time considering the change before acting (they call it *Contemplation*). As an executive, you spend a lot of time thinking about the change before acting. What's important is that you acknowledge that your employees will need some time to adjust! Remember that your thinking process, and the time you share planning with other executive team members may take months before you act; your people have not had that luxury. Expect a bit of shock or confusion.

II. Departments and Customers – Groups of people who receive the change

Not only will you introduce multiple kinds of changes, many different groups will be affected by the change, and this is an area where executives often underestimate the impact of a new change. Making the assumption that everyone knows is a serious error – making the assumption that everyone cares is even more serious! Almost all groups will be affected by change to some degree.

The groups fall into two categories: **direct involvement vs. on the fringe.**

a. People with direct involvement in the change

The major groups within an organization who are directly impacted by change include people on the front lines of manufacturing, mid-level managers and directors who must carry out the new initiative and make it part of their daily activity. Customer facing groups, in particular, are increasingly vulnerable to the impact of a change.

b. People on the fringes of the change

Tangential groups within an organization are also

affected by change. These groups may have only a slight connection with the project but, because they are still impacted, their influence can change the course of a deployment.

Either group can support or derail the change. Groups directly impacted by change can raise resistance and challenges because of the direct impact on their lives—especially those who are customer facing. Make no mistake—tangential groups at the fringes of the change can slow things down, and even bring change to a halt.

III. Team Level—Teams within your organization

Teams in your organization will be affected by change (Finance, Legal, HR, for example). Group dynamics (competition for resources between teams) can be positive if managed correctly during the change by pointing to the end goal; the purpose of the initiative. When resources are slim, projects are on overdrive, and teams are asked to supply their best people to the work, Architects need to ensure teams get the support they need when asked to add further project effort to their workload.

IV. Mid-level Leaders—The critical group who leads the change

Your leaders will make or break the effectiveness of the change. They need to lead with confidence, be visible, and communicate frequently and effectively. They need to be informed with a clear rationale for the change, and they need executive support—*especially* Middle Managers and Supervisors, who will bring their teams directly through the change. *Beware passive-aggressive behavior on their part; they may agree publically, but work to undermine the change privately.*

V. Individual Level—the 'led' on the ground floor

Without individual acceptance of the change, it will NOT become part of your organization. There's a LOT going on at the individual level—down to the level of brain chemistry, personal motivation, organizational citizenship, and employee engagement. **In short, the *entire* organization is impacted by your new initiative.**

You have the vantage point of understanding your culture; that is, the ways things get done in your organization. Armed with that knowledge and a blueprint for change, you can implement large scale change. Helping your organization respond effectively to the change is the reason you need an Architect's Blueprint.

So, here's a blueprint; a plan; the BIG PICTURE for managing change:

FINISHING THE CHANGE
The Nuts and Bolts of Change

SUPERSTRUCTURE LAUNCHING THE CHANGE	ARCHITECT BEHAVIORS	DAY-TO-DAY SUPPORT (WHAT TO EXPECT DURING CHANGE)
1. Selection of Team Leadership 2. Team Selection 3. Develop an Intentional Communication Plan 4. Detailed Project Plan 5. Team Cadence 6. Feedback Loop to Assure Communication 7. System Issues - Details for IT changes	Managing Organizational, Managerial and Individual Barriers to Completion 1. Persistence 2. Clarity 3. Recognition 4. Managerial Check-in 5. Communicating to the End 6. Renewing Team Vigor	1. Knowing that there are "changes within a change". 2. Understanding and Managing Change Resistance 3. Managing Team Drama

FOUNDATION PREPARING FOR THE CHANGE
1. Developing the Rationale
2. Conducting Due Diligence
3. Deliberately Planning Effective Communication
4. Defining Initial Metrics

GROUNDWORK
There's a lot going on during a major organizational initiative.

Here's a way to think about Change implementation: it's a lot like constructing a skyscraper. There's a foundation, a super-structure and a lot of nuts and bolts.

Change Foundation - What is it?

The foundation for the change is the *Rationale*. You make a decision to invoke a change for good, high-level reasons. Organizations have great needs that induce change. You take a leadership position, and decide to make the change for the good of the company. The Rationale for Change is communicated, financial investments are made, and human resources are committed.

Change Superstructure - What is it?

The superstructure is the logistical act of organizing for the change. Teams are assembled, charters are written, plans are engaged, and the rhythm of change process is committed. Materials are purchased, system programmers are engaged, training activities are put in place. A team leader is put in place, kick-off meetings are conducted, and the process begins to move. The physics of Change Management are slowly coming into place. There is less room for speculation and innovation. The plan is getting locked down.

Change Nuts and Bolts - What are they?

Change nuts and bolts are the details of successful change; the day-in, day-out management of the project, which includes lots, and lots, *and lots* of details. Without the nuts and bolts, a superstructure will crumble—sometimes crash. This is where the analogy between physics and change management unite. Without rivets, the superstructure fails; without details, the change fails. ***Details, details, details!***

Things like HR processes, reward systems, role definitions, process evaluation, data retrieval and storage—these are the details that can make or break the change.

While a strong foundation is essential, and a framework and superstructure are mandatory, it is the simple, tiny— yet critical—nuts and bolts of the change that do the biggest work (or cause the greatest failures), in the end. They hold the change together; they make it stick; they make it work; and, they make it stand.

Architects don't manage all the elements of building construction, but they *understand* them. As the Architect of Change, you want to ensure these elements are being well managed by someone in your organization.

So, we'll take each of these elements in greater detail in the sections that follow.

Real World Challenges:

STANDARDIZATION OF TECHNICIAN UNIFORMS

In a business setting, nothing is more personal to people than the clothes they wear—especially Technicians that pride themselves on looking a certain way. Yet, due to a merger, there was no standard uniform.

Simply telling technicians that they would be wearing new uniforms would not be effective. To engage these technicians, we found the likely sources of resistance and engaged them in the process, conducting a survey that yielded over 1,000 participants, who told us what they were concerned about. Access to the clothing, and ensuring it would fit well and be available when necessary, were among the great concerns, in addition to concerns about geographic differences in temperature and humidity, along with safety. The input from the technicians proved extremely valuable, and the details they provided made all the difference in acceptance of this change.

> "The secret of change is to focus all of your energy; not on fighting the old, but on building the new." *Socrates*

CHAPTER 3

PREPARING FOR THE CHANGE - THE FOUNDATION

FINISHING THE CHANGE
The Nuts and Bolts of Change

SUPERSTRUCTURE	DAY-TO-DAY SUPPORT
LAUNCHING THE CHANGE	(WHAT TO EXPECT DURING
1. Selection of Team Leadership	CHANGE)
2. Team Selection	1. Knowing that there are
3. Develop an Intentional	"changes within a change".
Communication Plan	2. Understanding and Managing
4. Detailed Project Plan	Change Resistance
5. Team Cadence	3. Managing Team Drama
6. Feedback Loop to Assure	
Communication	
7. System Issues - Details for	
IT changes	

FOUNDATION PREPARING FOR THE CHANGE
1. Developing the Rationale
2. Conducting Due Diligence
3. Deliberately Planning Effective Communication
4. Defining Initial Metrics

GROUNDWORK
There's a lot going on during a major organizational initiative.

An Architect wouldn't construct a skyscraper without considering the foundation, and you can't lead a change without a solid starting point.

We're making the assumption that you've already committed dollars to this endeavor. We're also making the assumption that your organizational leadership team has agreed upon the purpose for the initiative.

The foundation consists of four parts:

1. Developing the **Rationale**

2. Conducting **Due Diligence** (balancing change diagnosis with change action),

3. Deliberately planning **Effective Communication**

4. Defining Initial **Metrics**

1. Developing The Rationale for the Change

At the very bottom of any change is answering the question, "*Why*?" Developing this rationale *early* in the process is the critical starting point. What are the parts of the rationale?

- Why did we choose to make this change?

- Why is this group of people involved?

- What are the long term company benefits of the change?

- Why are we doing the change at this time?

You and your executive team must take the time and effort *to clearly and carefully think through the rationale of the change.*

2. Conduct Due Diligence: *Balancing* Change Diagnosis with Change Action

I recently completed an assignment that reminded me, once again, of the delicate balance between Change Action and Change Diagnosis. Here's what I mean:

Change Diagnosis is that set of actions we take to clearly and carefully understand and define the change. We conduct interviews with stakeholders, both high and low; near and far. We talk to technology team members to ensure we know the organizational impact of a new system. We conduct focus groups to check the pulse of the organization regarding the change. Finally, we gather data to determine issues of change resistance and the root causes of those issues.

Key elements of change diagnosis

1. Defining the scope and definition of the change, so everyone understands what's going on.

2. Understanding the kind of team needed to accomplish the change.

3. Who will be your "General Contractor?"

4. How do you plan to effectively communicate this change to your organization?

5. Which areas of your organization will be open to the change and which ones will oppose it?

Change Action is the launching and implementation of the change; taking all the designs and putting them into practice.

Key elements of change action

1. Developing a *precise* scope and rationale for the change.

2. Careful selection of the Change Team.

3. Communicating the Change Leader to the organization.

4. Development of two-way communication channels to ensure a feedback loop.

5. Management of the naysayers by assessing the greatest likelihood for resistance, and preemptively managing toward productive behavior.

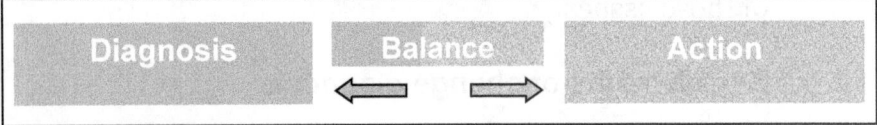

Too much diagnosis often leads to paralysis, which leads to non-action, which leads to participant cynicism. **Shoot-from-the-hip action** means a lack of preparedness, incomplete plans, and ineffective communication.

Here's the tricky part: Launching a change sometimes happens without the least bit of diagnosis (You've seen this and may be guilty of it!). Conversely, waiting too long to launch (and complete) a change will waste precious motivational energy. So, what to do? Ensure the key elements of the diagnosis are done thoroughly, but as quickly as possible. Once you act, finish the change as rapidly as possible.

Delaying change implementation allows people to ossify a position; that is, they start building psychological and structural barriers to prevent the change from happening. Move quickly, yet deliberately. That's the Golden Mean.

3. Deliberately planning for Effective *Intentional* Communication

Mark Twain wrote, "*A Classic is something everyone wants to have read, but no one wants to read.*" Communication is the one thing all organizations talk about, but few make the effort to ensure it occurs. People believe that communication is happening all the time, simply because people talk. Poor communication has an adverse impact on Change Management effectiveness. When people do not understand each other, they make costly mistakes.

What's the executive role in communicating change? You're not developing the actual communication at this point, but you are ensuring someone has the responsibility to get this done.

4. Defining Initial metrics

Without a clear set of metrics at the beginning of the change, you won't know if you're making progress along the way, and you surely won't know if you changed what you planned to change. This takes effort!

Ensure you're part of the team developing those metrics, because you're going to check on them as the project moves along. Every change you induce requires different metrics, but don't develop so many you can't track them all. Too much detailed reporting takes away precious time from actual project management. Use these questions to guide your thinking:

1. *What really matters when this is all said and done? What do we really want to impact?*

2. *What's worth taking the time, effort and employee motivation to collect the data?*

3. *How will you judge the success of the project? Financial metrics? Behavioral metrics (do people do things differently than they did before?)? Compliance metrics?*

4. *What do you really want to be different?*

5. *What measures will tell you if you've turned the corner?*

6. *What data will you have to recognize people?*

Summary: *The change foundation is critical for future success. Take the time to do it right.*

"If you do not change direction, you may end up where you are heading." Loa Tzu

CHAPTER 4

THE ROLE OF THE ARCHITECT DURING CHANGE

You take on different personae as you lead your initiative. Some of these will be more natural to you, based on your experience and personality, but all are valid.

The Architect's Persona during Change—
Strategic Evangelist

Architect's Persona During Change

- **Strategic Evangelist**

- **Chess Master**

- **Great Communicator**

- **Organizational Psychologist**

- **Five Star General**

- **Organizational Diplomat**

Executives are sometimes seen as cool-headed, unfeeling Spock-like figures, and the notion of the impassioned evangelist seeking to win the hearts of his or her hearers may seem out of character for many. In truth, personality is difficult to change, but the ability to publicly express a deep desire to make a change is within the reach of any executive.

As an evangelistic leader, you inspire the team to go forward. The evangelist is the passionate inspirer of those who would follow.

The evangelist shows a future others cannot see, and encourages them to join the journey. The evangelist asks people to turn away from their current ways to do something entirely new. In short, they ask people to change.

As an Architect, you need to understand the change so well that you are immersed in the rationale for the change. You feel it, breathe it, sense it and know exactly why it is necessary for your organization—*and* you're willing to launch it while the business is conducting day-to-day operations. If *you* don't believe in it, no one else will.

The Architect's Persona during Change—*Chess Master*

Great chess masters develop skills to coordinate multiple pieces toward a final outcome. They have plans within plans to anticipate the movements of an opponent, with the ultimate goal of winning the day. Every move is timed in concert with other moves to achieve victory. Some moves are anticipated far in advance allow for success at just the right moment.

As a chess master, you need to coordinate high level, strategic activities, ensuring clarity between initiatives, toward an end goal. As a chess master, you need to ensure that the various actions within your organization are well-timed to achieve the change you seek. Architects need to display the persona of a chess master during organizational change for the following reasons:

1. Every organization has MULTIPLE strategic actions going on at any given point in time. The vantage point of the chess master is to see the parts working in concert for organizational good. Architects coordinate organizational linkages!

2. FEW in the organization have the power to move various pieces at will, but executives can do so when needed for the greater good of the change.

3. An executive can tap the intelligence and capability of many feet on the ground, allowing for a strong vantage point during change, as opposed to those with a departmental or divisional view.

4. At the highest levels in organizations, people are jockeying for position like knights and bishops and rooks; only an executive can choose whether to use them or not use them at certain points in time. All are powerful, but not all are necessary at the same time.

Organizational change is a great 'chess game.' When Architects help their teams coordinate action, block adversarial barriers, and ensure good timing, the game can be won with great satisfaction; but, it requires discipline, concentration, and intentionality. Change requires constant Architect focus.

The Architect's Persona during Change—
Great Communicator

During a major organizational change, everything is up in the air. What was once stable has moved; what was predictable is uncertain; what was easy becomes hard–at least for a while. Instability is tough on organizations, and it often leads to employee frustration and inaction, as they wait to know what's happening. Trusted, credible leaders are the answer to the chaos.

As the great communicator, Architects ensure the following things are understood among the masses:

1. The rationale for the change is cleared and carefully articulated to all, again and again – and again!

2. People know when things are taking place, who will be responsible to lead the change team and who has answers to day-to-day questions.

3. When things break (and they inevitably do), the great communicator explains where things are at, what's being done to correct the problem and who is responsible to complete the actions.

4. Most importantly, the great communicator 'stays the course' throughout the change, continually providing presence of leadership as the project moves forward.

Everyone knows communication is important during change, but the great communicator makes it an art form which, in the end, serves to help the organization adjust to new things.

The Architect's Persona during Change—
Organizational Psychologist

I once counseled a Senior Vice President who failed to effectively communicate the impact of a change to his people. When they discovered what was happening, he nearly had an uprising on his hands. Although *he* was comfortable with the change, he had not anticipated the reactions of the people when the change was introduced. Had he considered the situation from their point of view, he could have managed things much differently, with much different results.

Change induces emotional reactions in organizations. Sometimes people feel threatened and fearful, sometimes they are angry, sometimes frustrated and disheartened. Employees are not unfeeling beings who act "Spock-like" in pure logic during change. They react with fear and, sometimes, anger. They are influenced by their own concerns of how the change will affect their role and their reporting structure. People wonder about the impact of the change to their personal lives outside of work, since change can alter schedules, working arrangements and, ultimately, impact their families, hobbies, and even something as simple as commuting time and where they will park their cars!

So, what element of executive persona addresses this issue of emotional reaction to change? Whether we like it or not, Architects need to respond to people as emotional beings, not just employees who need to "adapt or leave." You need to act the role of organizational psychologist, one who hears the needs of a client (the organization) and responds therapeutically and wisely to help people adjust to new things.

You act as an organizational psychologist by helping people adapt to the change; by listening to concerns and offering creative and effective counsel.

Not all Architects will have this ability, but the best executives will understand that it is necessary for people to be heard, and ensures that people get a chance to express their voice about the impact of the change.

Wisdom from an Architect during a time of change can calm a situation and bring order out of chaos. Insight from an executive during a time of change can help people understand the value of their struggle and the long term benefits of working through a change. In short, you can help people grow emotionally during a change, producing stronger employees and a stronger organization when the change is complete.

The Architect's Persona during Change—
Five Star General

The notion of a helmeted George Patton leading change may be off-putting to most readers, since we are at an enlightened stage of management theory that portrays leaders as engaging and transparent; averse to abuses of power. Most would agree that unchecked power can cause more harm than good.

Yet, during change, there are times for you to act as a five star general. Military leaders at the highest levels decide where artillery, logistics, and manpower will be applied in a situation. Military leaders at the highest levels assess a situation, pull together the strategy of multiple moving parts, and call for decisive action to win a battle. *This is especially true when things start to go wrong.*

Coordinating Resources

Here's how the analogy holds: during organizational change, many different sources of energy, power, leadership and tactics must be pulled together to ensure the change becomes part of the organizational DNA. A leader who seeks the best for the organization takes command at certain points in a project to do what others cannot – martial (forgive the pun) resources to complete the task.

Staying the Course

When others start to give up, the person in command continues to press forward, knowing the outcome. I recall a meeting where one leader said, "Leaders who drop their shoulders when things get tough lose the respect of their teams." What he meant was this: the leader must maintain courage in the face of struggle because people are watching. During organizational change, the entire organization will be under stress, under pressure, and under strain. Strong leaders recognize this and continue to 'show the way,' without faltering in the mission. Organizations going through IT/System changes are especially vulnerable to a weakness in the ranks. Strong Architects know this to be true, and they continue to show the way when others are losing heart.

Managing Obstacles

Military operations face strange and unexpected obstacles, including weather, terrain, disease, and lack of supplies. Unless they are managed, these obstacles can have a major impact on the outcome of the goal. Architects help the team stay the course in the face of struggle and unforeseen consequences. They use their teams to assess the obstacle (best done ahead of time, by the way) and find ways to overcome the challenge.

Taking command when necessary

The five star general persona must be used sparingly; it is an aspect of the executive personality during change. When the situation calls for decisive action during a major change, executives must take command.

The Architect's Persona during Change—
Organizational Diplomat

Whether we like it or not, organizational change creates winners and losers (anyone who says otherwise speaks from ignorance of the impact of change). Change sometimes causes unforeseen losses for some, and those losses can be a major force in the resistance of the change. In other circumstances, people may gain new influence, greater power and increased control because of an organizational change. Whether we like it or not, those circumstances can lead to the very basic human reactions of jealousy and envy. *Issues of justice and fairness are often at the bottom of resistance to organizational change.*

A bruised ego is often collateral damage during change. While professionals may hide their reactions, emotional reactions are part of Change Management, and that's where executives need to take on the persona of an organizational diplomat.

The history of organizations is the history of human nature

The history of the world is rife with countries, clans, nations, empires winning and losing territory, natural resources, status and power. The history of the world is packed with fair and unfair exchanges with long-term impact.

Diplomacy is required during organizational change

At a much smaller, but no less meaningful, scale, organizational leadership wins and loses ground during times of change. As great diplomats bring skills to the table to calm fears, adjust borders, tame the agitators, and find a fair and equitable solution for all, so too must executives find ways to improve unpleasant and difficult situations arising from change. Organizational change is tough, and a strong executive understands their role in soothing egos, smoothing rough edges, and helping cooler heads to prevail.

Why this is a critical skill during organizational change

Architects must take on this role because of the long-term impact of an organizational change. **It's easy to win one battle** with a peer or department and tell them to "Just do it," but over the long haul (and this is true of the history of the world), resentments build, departments become siloed to protect their turf, and organizational memories are stored in the memories of leaders who lost. Diplomacy is a necessary skill during change for the long-term survival and effectiveness of the organization.

Summary: *You may have one or more of these skill-sets, or they may be part of your team skill-sets; candidly, these skill-sets are common in general management! What's important is that you understand the need to apply these personae at the right time to help the team succeed.*

"One reason people resist change is that they focus on what they have to give up, rather than what they have to gain." *Rick Godwin*

Chapter 5

Launching the Change - The Superstructure

FINISHING THE CHANGE
The Nuts and Bolts of Change

SUPERSTRUCTURE **LAUNCHING THE CHANGE**	DAY-TO-DAY SUPPORT (WHAT TO EXPECT DURING CHANGE)
1. Selection of Team Leadership	
2. Team Selection	1. Knowing that there are
3. Develop an Intentional	"changes within a change".
Communication Plan	2. Understanding and Managing
4. Detailed Project Plan	Change Resistance
5. Team Cadence	3. Managing Team Drama
6. Feedback Loop to Assure	
Communication	
7. System Issues - Details for	
IT changes	

FOUNDATION PREPARING FOR THE CHANGE
1. Developing the Rationale
2. Conducting Due Diligence
3. Deliberately Planning Effective Communication
4. Defining Initial Metrics

GROUNDWORK
There's a lot going on during a major organizational initiative.

So, we have a foundation consisting of a rationale, due diligence, communications, and metrics. You also have a sense of the different personae you project to effectively manage a change.

Let's move on to what it takes to launch the change, to construct the superstructure of the building–the framework of the initiative. The more seriously you take these elements of the launch, the more likely they are to get done. Think of the steel girders that rise during a skyscraper build. Things are taking shape. Here are the elements necessary to successfully launch a change.

1. **Selection of Team Leadership**

2. **Team Selection**

3. **Develop an Intentional Communication Plan**

4. **Detailed Project Plan**

5. **Team Cadence**

6. **Feedback Loop to Assure Communication**

7. **System Issues – Details for IT changes**

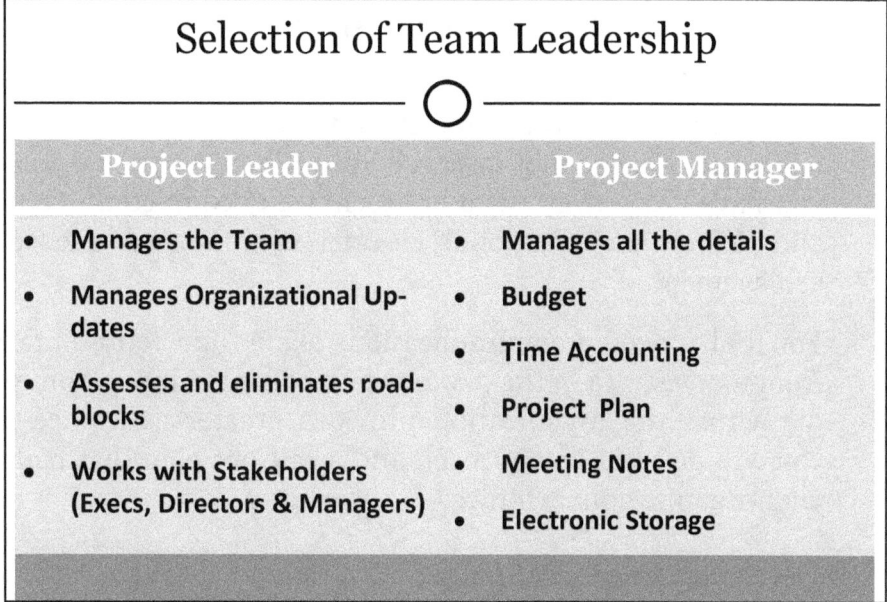

Figure 4 – Difference between project leader and project manager.

Selection of Team Leadership—Accountability

You'll need two people – one to lead the team, and one to manage the details. You'll need one to break down barriers and roadblocks, and another to ensure the roadblocks are gone; one to communicate to everyone, and one to ensure all communications are properly stored for quick access; one to keep the team on track, and one to keep track of the team. It's important that the Project Manager reports into the Project Leader. Choose a leader who will stay the course until the last 'i' is dotted and the last 't' is crossed!

Team Selection is a critical moment for the project

While your role is not to lead the team, you clearly want input into the development of the team, since team membership is a deal breaker for most change efforts. The wrong team can bring the change to a halt, or at least slow it dramatically. You need the best your organization can bring. As the leader of the entire effort, your judgment, your input and your ability to bring the right   resources to the team make all the difference.

Do not use the "B" team simply because they are available.

One of the easiest ways to bring a team together is to use the "B" team, because they are available. Whatever you do, ensure you have "A" players who are technically competent, capable and *driven* organizational citizens with a track record of achievement.

You'll also need a communications leader and representation from many strata of the organization. Gaining input from people across the organization provides greater assurance that you will develop an approach and a roll-out plan that truly fit your organizational culture.

Team Selection

○

Title	Role
• Communications Lead	• Manages all communications details
• Organizational Representation	• Team members who are a voice for all organizational strata
• Additional as required (Example: IT Lead)	• Team members essential to implementation

Figure 5 – Selection of team members.

Development of an Intentional Communications Plan

Communication is one of those overused, hackneyed words because it's important. What's more important is ensuring your team has a plan for intentional communications. To give you a sense of what's required, take a look at Figure 6.

Figure 6 - The elements of an effective, intentional communication plan during change.

This is the work of your communications lead–helping you to be successful as you support the project. A strong communications leader will be very savvy about the elements shown in

Figure 6. They're all necessary as you launch and support a new initiative.

Detailed project plan

As I mentioned above, executives need to know and assure that there is ONE individual who knows all the cost, timing, details, details, and more details of the project—and who updates it every day! That's the project manager. The person who manages the "GO LIVE" dates; the one who knows every possible detail about how the project is proceeding. **Do not initiate a major change initiative without one of these critical team members.**

Establish Team Cadence

Ensure there is a standard protocol for updates at every level. Set this expectation upon the very start of the project. The initial meeting is the time to say, "We're going to meet every week until this is done." This cadence becomes a dependable mile marker for every member of the team. There is significant psychological assurance that comes from a dependable schedule.

Feedback Loop

Do not risk hearing about the success (or failure) of your project too far down the road! Build an intentional feedback loop, so you know what's going on. Early and immediate (useful) feedback helps steer the change.

*System Issues for an IT Project (special circumstance of change) [See Appendix B].

Summary: *Launching the change means ensuring everything is in place to effectively begin the project. Work done well at this point will pay off down the road; but a lack of attention to detail and effort in the beginning can cause major disasters as the project gains momentum.*

Real World Challenges:

MANAGING EMPLOYEE CONCERNS DURING A MERGER

During a merger, some employees had concerns about the rationale behind the joining of two organizations. What they did know was this: the other guys had the same skill they had, and thus both groups were certain the other group was going to take their jobs. Through some direct work out in the field with the employees, this issue was brought to executive management in the combined organization, who wrote letters directly to the employees to assure them they would be retained, thus avoiding confusion and the potential loss of employees. The rationale for the change—that of complimentary technology and complimentary geographic dispersion and product offerings—was made clear, avoiding a crisis. The quick action of leadership during the change made the difference.

"Nothing is so painful to the human mind as a great and sudden change." *Mary Shelley, Frankenstein*

CHAPTER 6

DAY-TO-DAY SUPPORT

WHAT TO EXPECT DURING CHANGE

FINISHING THE CHANGE		
The Nuts and Bolts of Change		

SUPERSTRUCTURE LAUNCHING THE CHANGE		DAY-TO-DAY SUPPORT (WHAT TO EXPECT DURING CHANGE)
1. Selection of Team Leadership 2. Team Selection 3. Develop an Intentional Communication Plan 4. Detailed Project Plan 5. Team Cadence 6. Feedback Loop to Assure Communication 7. System Issues - Details for IT changes		1. Knowing that there are "changes within a change". 2. Understanding and Managing Change Resistance 3. Managing Team Drama

FOUNDATION PREPARING FOR THE CHANGE
1. Developing the Rationale 2. Conducting Due Diligence 3. Deliberately Planning Effective Communication 4. Defining Initial Metrics

GROUNDWORK
There's a lot going on during a major organizational initiative.

Once the change is underway, there are two critical things you can expect, and one thing that may happen. You'll need to be attentive to them all.

1. *Knowing that there are changes hidden within a "change"*

2. *Understanding and Managing Change Resistance*

3. *Managing Change Team Drama*

1) There are changes hidden within the "change"

It seems logical that leaders would understand the 'pool table' effect of a change—one thing impacts another—but, very often, managers and executives fail to see the deeper complexity of changes within a change. For example: a company decides to use a new software for their HR systems. For most people, this will be perceived as an IT/System change, BUT! The cognitive changes required at the employee level (new thinking, learning, training), managerial level (new metrics, processes, reporting and workflow) and executive level (increased expectations for data access, improved performance metrics and rapid assessment of issues) are part of what I call the *changes within the change*.

Simply think of how difficult it is to learn a simple, new software package without assistance, and you'll see what I mean. Here are some examples of tensions within a change. Based on their role in the company, you'll have people of all stripes focusing on different elements of these tensions (and they will focus very hard on the things that most affects them and their teams or departments)—you need to stay above the fray and continually remind people of the goal.

Significant Tensions *within* a Change	
Respect the past	Embrace the future
We've always done "it" this way	We need to do "this" a new way
It was a lot easier back then	We have to learn something new
Centralization	Decentralization
Team needs	Organizational demands
Individual expectations	Organizational expectations
Frontline employee viewpoints	Executive viewpoints
Operational priorities	Change project priorities

Figure 7 – Tensions within a change.

Many of these elements are present with every change—these are the tensions hidden deep below the surface, and each one requires explanation, understanding, and resolution. You'll often find someone who is adamant about one or two of these elements who simply cannot see the whole picture. Sometimes people are able to resolves these issues on their own but, very likely, they will require assistance in sorting out these tensions. As an Architect, you want to know that someone is thinking about these issues and managing them appropriately.

How does the Architect of Change help to resolve these tensions?

The human brain forces out unwanted and useless information in the quest for a goal. Architects who carefully articulate the *raison d'être* for the change are miles ahead in their change management efforts. "Knowing where we're going" is a big deal, since a clear direction removes other decision options.

Think for a moment about moving from one place to another. Maybe you did that as a kid. Your parents had thought about it for months, then sprung the news on you! You were confused, angry, frustrated, sad and disoriented. After the move, you were wary, concerned, cautious and hesitant. That's change management in a nutshell.

2) Managing Change Resistance

This issue is brought up again and again as a source of change failure and, thankfully, is receiving some academic attention, since resistance to change is not always a malicious attempt to derail an initiative. Resistance is more complex than people who say, "I don't want to do this." Executives play a **major role** in managing resistance. Understand that working *with* natural human autonomy is far more effective than forcing people to act.

The heart of the change resistance

We have all heard the well-worn phrase, "Winning hearts and minds," as a recommendation for effectively managing change, but there is little detail behind that phrase. Though there are endless pages written about Change Management, the nuts and bolts of why people resist change are rarely examined in detail. Leaders may or may not want to address them all, since some of them are very personal, but simply understanding these basic (and, in many cases, legitimate) reasons for resistance may be one of the best things leaders can grasp in their quest for change.

Leader perspective: "It's your job."

Leaders may believe that the unwritten contract between the organization and the employee allows for pressure to make changes as needed. "I pay you, therefore I can make the rules." Agreed ... but ... the social contract someone writes when they sign on is built around a set of psychological assumptions of job role, commitment, longevity, etc. When the rules change, people's lives change, and you'll hear them say, "This isn't what I signed up for!".

In a world driven by non-stop demands and constant social media interruption, people desire some form of predictability to allow them to manage their lives. While organizational change presents opportunities, it also presents risk; risk to schedules, to families, to relationships with co-workers, and to comfortable surroundings.

Perspective of people in the trenches—Upsetting the Apple Cart of Status Quo

People like (and need) predictability. People build their lives around a predictable pattern that allows them to do other things they enjoy. Unpredictability creates fear—right down to the neurological level. Research shows that the brain must work harder with uncertainty, causing a reaction to the novel situation which requires more effort and more energy to manage. The word stasis is a word used in biology to describe an ideal condition for human flourishing for a reason.

Fear of personal loss

People could (or are going to) lose their jobs. Every time I have worked on a major change, this is the first question that arises: "Will I still have a job when this change is complete?"

People could possibly change roles. Sometimes organizational changes introduce unpredictability in changing roles. People run the risk of losing positions they have striven to achieve. Organization changes can throw their designs into chaos.

Concern about Organizational Discomfort

People may end up working for someone they don't like. Much research has been written on the importance of the direct manager or supervisor as the key to employment happiness. Working for someone we don't like, or someone who has a poor reputation, causes people to be uneasy— and sometimes to start looking for other jobs.

People will be relocated. Sometimes the relocation can be as simple as across the street, while other times it can be across the world. People's lives are impacted when a major organizational change is underway.

Organizational Losses

People are going to lose something they value–friendships, location, office space. Some employee engagement surveys ask questions about whether people 'have a friend at work.' The point is this: people come to know others in a significant and sometimes personal way, developing deep friendships that can be changed in an instant when the news of change is in the wind.

Then there is loss of organizational prestige. Those who once had power, large teams, and significant influence can lose their influence in a heartbeat. Their reactions are always one of loss, fear, and sometimes bitterness and anger. The literature on organizational justice may not be common reading to most leaders, but perceived unfairness can create not only unwilling staff, but can generate the naysayers—those interested in seeing the change fail.

Expenditure of Effort and Limited Energy

People have to learn new things. Learning takes effort. Effort is costly in terms of cognitive expenditure and emotional investment. While learning creates interesting and fun opportunities, it still increases demand on busy people.

People may have to expend much energy they don't currently have to give. People are stressed out in their roles, and the addition of yet more work to their already busy schedules can cause concern. Whilst some may enjoy the additional adrenaline rush of yet more engagement in the organizational process of change, the majority of people are already maxed out, and the notion of yet another project can be overwhelming.

Fear of discovery

People may be hiding things they don't want others to discover! In some cases, people are fearful of discovery. I recall one man telling me something very abrupt when I interviewed him about a pending change. I asked, "How can we help you?" His answer, "Just leave us alone." He had something to hide.

People may become incompetent in their role. It is conceivable that a new software system or new series of processes may simply cause someone's skills to become outdated, causing them great alarm if they sense they will not be able to adjust to their new role. People coming into an office environment after being in the field are often vulnerable to this concern.

What is the role of the Architect in managing resistance?

While it is true that these concerns are personal and will require personal effort on the part of those who are 'changed,' leaders cannot simply dismiss these things as nonsensical concerns that people should just accept.

The following are some common executive approaches to managing change resistance. Leaders believe that the unwritten contract between the organization and the employee allows for pressure to make changes as needed, but here's a hint: Command and Control is rarely helpful.

The wrong approach

- "Do this or you'll be fired." I begin with the least helpful of the approaches.

- "Upper management insists that we do this." This is the weak leader's approach to getting people to comply.

> **CAUTION:**
>
> Be careful not to be part of the resistance problem. Don't unnecessarily create resistance by forcing an action that could be chosen if it were properly explained!

- "Just get on board."

- "You're not a team player." This is organizational extortion.

- "Why don't you get it?" Translation: "You're an idiot".

The reasons leaders use these approaches?

- A lack of leadership patience.

- Pressure from those up above.

- Market pressures.

- A personal sense of "I did it, why can't you?"

- A belief that the change should be obvious to followers.

> **CHANGE TIP**
> Managing Resistance
>
> *You have the opportunity to stuff it down their throats, or bring them along.*
>
> **Steve Meyers, Vivint**

Some reminders:

- Remember: As I mentioned in the first section, you and your executive team have been thinking about this change for months—maybe years—and then, out of the blue, you announce the change and expect others to jump on board.

- "Just do it" may be helpful for exercise, but it doesn't play well with people whose lives are going to be upset because of a change.

- Sometimes, naysayers actually have a point. Ignoring them only creates enemies and hostile compliance.

- Sometimes, executives think people at lower levels of an organization should just 'do' stuff.

- Sometimes, the change causes serious disruption in people's lives!

- Bohn's Law of Change: "If you push, people shove."

Maybe there's a better way to manage resistance.

The best way to manage resistance is to manage it from the beginning of the project, but projects take time; things happen and things ... well, things change! So, here are some tips to manage resistance after the project is underway.

- Sometimes resistance happens because the project is 'going south.' Things aren't working as planned, and executives want to hide the obvious. At this point, honesty during change is the key to credibility. If things are going wrong, admit it. No need to sugar coat things when people know there are obvious problems. Leaders lose credibility when they ignore or run away from obvious, known problems.

- The simple act of listening provides a great deal of credibility with people. That doesn't mean hours of cathartic soul searching in a dimly lit room—it means taking the time to deliberately hear what people have to say. Let people vent for a bit.

- Sometimes, jujitsu is necessary. Sometimes we need to use the power of the negative to make gains. Working with the naysayers and bringing them into the project is more powerful than resisting their every complaint.

- Above all, having a clear and compelling argument for the change is essential to persuade users who may be resisting the change. A compelling argument requires clear language and cogent statistics to overcome the naysayers.

*When you absolutely **must** deal with resistance head on.*

You've prepared people, you've communicated, you've listened and planned, but there are still 'rebels without a cause' within your ranks. You need their effort, or you need their exit. Here are a few specific things you can do to manage resistance head on.

1. Tell team members privately: The train is leaving the station—you have an opportunity to get on board, or not.

2. Reassign them to different roles.

3. Engage them in the change team where possible to improve their participation.

4. Remove them from the project entirely.

5. Accept that some will not need to do things the new way.

What to do when things go wrong.

One simple fact of managing change is this: While you may plan well, developing and selecting the best team, and engage all the leadership necessary to ensure a good outcome, things will go wrong. It's simply not possible to manage all the possible variants of what could take place.

Bottom line: Honest and accurate reflection of the situation is the best way to manage a struggling project. The Architect goes straight at the problem and tackles it head-on, without blaming, but engaging the entire team in the solution. Acting as though there is no problem is as much a danger as overreacting to the situation. Think *Organizational Psychologist*—calming people down whilst still moving toward a solution.

3) Managing Change Team Drama

Sometimes you'll need to manage stress and tension on the change team by reminding them of the overall goal. Teams get stressed out! Why does the Architect need to be involved in managing team drama? You have the ability to refocus the team, and your level of authority will show them the value you're putting on resolving the issue and getting on with the project. In the end, they're accountable to you.

What to Expect During Change

○

Changes Within a Change

- Remember to see the whole picture
- Expect the 'Pool Table' effect of any change
- Balance employee needs with organizational needs
- Know where you're going

Managing Change Resistance

- Recognize employee risk with organizational changes
- Involve employees in the change as much as possible
- Remember Bohn's Law: "If you push, people shove"

Managing Change Drama

- Bring the focus back to the original goal

Figure 8 – What to expect during change

> "They always say time changes things, but you actually have to change them yourself."   *Andy Warhol*

CHAPTER 7

FINISHING THE CHANGE: THE NUTS AND BOLTS

FINISHING THE CHANGE
The Nuts and Bolts of Change

SUPERSTRUCTURE	ARCHITECT BEHAVIORS	DAY-TO-DAY SUPPORT
LAUNCHING THE CHANGE		(WHAT TO EXPECT DURING CHANGE)
1. Selection of Team Leadership	Managing Organizational, Managerial and Individual Barriers to Completion	1. Knowing that there are "changes within a change".
2. Team Selection	1. Persistence	2. Understanding and Managing Change Resistance
3. Develop an Intentional Communication Plan	2. Clarity	3. Managing Team Drama
4. Detailed Project Plan	3. Recognition	
5. Team Cadence	4. Managerial Check-in	
6. Feedback Loop to Assure Communication	5. Communicating to the End	
7. System Issues - Details for IT changes	6. Renewing Team Vigor	

FOUNDATION PREPARING FOR THE CHANGE
1. Developing the Rationale
2. Conducting Due Diligence
3. Deliberately Planning Effective Communication
4. Defining Initial Metrics

GROUNDWORK
There's a lot going on during a major organizational initiative.

Real World Challenges:

IMPROVING CUSTOMER SERVICE THROUGH METRICS

Transforming a struggling team into world class service providers

A customer service team struggled mightily, seeking support from the organization for technology and support, but to no avail. No one listened. The complaints from the team were simply anecdotal, and lacking anything except emotional substance.

By using a set of simple, but clear, metrics, the managers of the department were able to convince upper management of the need for technology and additional staff. The metrics included customer dissatisfaction reports for call waiting times and benchmarking against other world class centers to show the deltas.

After the metrics were made known, the executives were able to understand the problem and lend support; ultimately allowing the customer service team to win the highest award in the company. Educating the executives with data was the key to making the change.

Finishing the change: the most difficult aspect of the process.

By far the toughest part of your work will be to finish the change and ensure it has been built into your organizational DNA. Finishing the details are the hardest, but most critical, part of change. It means managing organizational, managerial and individual barriers to completion. You wouldn't want a building without a roof, and you don't want a change partially completed. You need to manage barriers with leadership behavior.

Three barriers to finishing the change: Organizational, Managerial and Individual

Organizational Barriers

1. *Unforeseen circumstances* Loss of resources is a sure-fire way to prevent the change from becoming part of the organization. Ensuring that the team has every-thing they need to finish the project should be a key concern for you and your team.

2. *Organizational Attention Deficit Disorder* Distractions can seriously hinder the completion of a change. Watch out for the new shiny object and avoid it!

Managerial Barriers

1. *Other priorities take the leader away from the project* When managers see the leader leave, it's a drain on morale.

2. *Boredom on the part of the leader* The simplest way to have others lose interest in a critical change project is when the leader moves on to something else.

3. **Leader mistakenly assumes the project is done**
This is a misguided action on the part of the leader. You need to know categorically that the project is done, done, done!

Individual Barriers

1. **Frustration—the 'grind' of the project** The long term expenditure of physical, mental, cognitive and emotional energy causes people to lose hope and lose heart. In short, they get tired of working on the project. Setbacks are particularly tough on team members, especially setbacks that could have been avoided through better upfront diagnosis.

   HINT: Energy lost must be energy replaced!

2. **Distraction** Shiny new objects are the bane of all projects, for the project, itself, was once a shiny new object! Individuals can get very distracted with emails, tweets, Facebook, and other social media. When the project becomes tedious, almost anything will lead to distraction.

Your behavioral role in finishing the change

Knowing that these barriers are very real, there are some distinct leadership skills you must consistently apply.

✓ **Persistence** As you read previously in the leader's role in change, you are leading the initiative in more ways than just through verbal communication. Persistence is omnipotent in the business world. People know that when the leader stays the course to the end, their leadership meant business—in other words, the change mattered to them. If the change matters to you, the leader, it will matter to your organization.

✓ *Clarity* Reminding people of the "why?" Constant clarity throughout the project, but especially at the end, makes all the difference; here's why we started this, here's why we're working on this, here's the difference it is already making, here's what it will do for our company.

✓ *Recognition*   Energy expended must be energy refilled. When the team works hard and gets things done, the leader must respond in kind: with hard work for the team! A bit of a party is always a good encouragement along the way— better still, have pizza with the team.

✓ *Team Check-in* Have the occasional brown bag lunch to ask, "What's happening within your group?   Are things proceeding as expected?" The secret is not to punish your leaders if things sound like they're going wrong at the grass roots level. Nothing is ever perfect in the beginning; how- ever, should you hear something good—well then—it's time for a celebration!

✓ *Communication to the end* Demonstrate what has hap- pened as a result of their effort! Tell the organization, tell the managers, tell the people the results of the team effort.

✓ *Renewing vigor through careful workload management* Don't add work to the already busy team members, but show them some care along the way–they need it! The best way I have seen this done is when an executive comes out to have lunch with a team to discuss progress.

How will you know when you're finished?

"Are we there yet?" the small child asks. You won't know if you're done until you hear it from people who have lived through the change and came out smiling (or, at least, grudg- ingly excited!).

It's not the foundation of a change that causes the project to weaken as the superstructure rises; it is the nuts and bolts that make all the difference. In short, details matter during a change. There is no way around it, but executives tend to avoid critical details during change.

Initial Metrics—how will we know? Remember those metrics you put in place at the beginning? Now is the time to test your theory.

Senior Management Check-in Have a meeting with your high level leaders, and ask them if they're satisfied with the outcome. Have a face-to-face check-in to assess how things are going.

Celebrate! When it's all said and done, celebrate! Make a big deal out of the success and the people who made it successful, because you may have to call on them in the future!

Summary: *So, as you've seen, change is far more complex, and it influences more facets of your organization, than you may have imagined before your read this book. Yet, as an executive–as the* **Architect of Change**—*you can establish a strong foundation, effectively launch a project, sustain it through ups and downs, and ensure the change will come to completion. It's up to you.*

Now, let's consider these elements in a case format:

CASE STUDY: PUTTING IT ALL TOGETHER

This is what change looks like once it's underway.   In the reflection sections, ask yourself what you would do to keep the change on track.

Background

Catalyst Medical Systems

Catalyst Medical Systems was developed in 1992 to provide post-surgical care for complex pediatric joint fractures. The repair of pediatric joint damage is made complex by growth plates, which must be properly managed as the joint is healed. Through years of research, Catalyst pioneer, Dr. Miriam Alexander, developed the technology and was appointed to Chief Executive Officer by the Board of Directors in 2010.

Catalyst sales offices are distributed across the globe, serving 27 countries on four continents, including South America, North America, Europe and Africa.

Brewster Medical Devices	Catalyst Medical Systems	DuCharme Industries
250 Employees	500 Employees	1,000 Employees
Est. 1975	Est. 1992	Est. 2009
100 m Euros	178 m Euros	250 m Euros

Brewster Medical Devices

This organization competed with Catalyst until last year, when Catalyst Medical Systems acquired them and their advanced technology for pediatric joint replacement. Brewster was headquartered in London, but in 2013, they moved their primary offices to Johannesburg to support the expanding African markets. William Tenwirth had been Chief Executive Officer of Brewster since it's inaugural production in 1975.

DuCharme Industries

DuCharme has rapidly become a major competitor to Catalyst, and recently developed a biomedical system that speeds recovery for pediatric patients by 18% over existing methods.

"SOMETHING NEEDS TO CHANGE"

Dr. Miriam Alexander, president of Catalyst Industries, looked deeply concerned as she stared out her office window. William Tenwirth, her CFO, and Jonathan Smith, her COO, were sitting across from her. They heard a knock at the door.

"Good morning Dr. Alexander," a voice sounded from outside her door. It was Tina Vasquez, Global VP of Sales.

"Hello Tina, I'm glad you're here," Dr. Alexander responded. "Thanks for coming on such short notice. I saw the latest monthly reports. Is it accurate that we're down 12% business year-over-year? What's the source of this issue? Why are we losing business to our competitors?"

Tina nodded, "Our competition argues that CATALYST has no true centralized systems for technical support. That fact has caused sales losses in several major competitive situations. When global customers ask us whether we can take calls and support anywhere, the ultimate answer is 'no.'"

Dr. Alexander was a medical expert, not an operations specialist. "Well, what can be done? Clearly we're not the only organization in the world that has faced this issue."

Jonathan Smith, VP Operations, made a recommendation. "We could install a centralized system for global support. There are many tools available today. Corporations do this all the time—we simply grew too fast with our acquisitions."

Dr. Alexander turned to her CFO, William Tenwirth: "William, we have funds in capital planning for this year."

"Yes," he answered abruptly, "and I agree we need a system. In fact, my old company, Brewster, had an excellent system for tracking, support and parts ordering. I'm not sure why *you've* never invested in a global system, but I need to remind you that those funds are for R&D and facility maintenance."

Dr. Alexander responded, "Jonathan, let's get this started. You have the lead for now, but I want to meet together in one week."

As she adjourned the meeting, Dr. Alexander asked Tina Vasquez, "Do you think this will solve the problem we're facing?"

Tina responded, "I think it will make a major difference. I will inform my sales team today."

"Then let's make this change happen. Jonathan, you have the lead. Give me monthly reports."

Preparing for the Change

* * * One Week Later * * *

Miriam Alexander was filled with expectation as the team filed into the conference room for the follow-up meeting.

CFO William Tenwirth was there, along with Jonathan Smith, VP-Ops, Tina Vasquez, VP Sales and Andrea Beauchamp, Chief Researcher. They were joined by Torva Karachenko, the customer service manager in Dallas, TX.

Jonathan Smith opened the meeting. "We have good news for you, Dr. Alexander. We started to assemble a team of several people in the UK with participation from IT, Sourcing and Operations. We've chosen an off-the-shelf package from Navigator Software for logging technical support calls, and hired Luke Stinson from Navigator as the project leader. Navigator is headquartered in the US."

At first, Dr. Alexander was elated, thinking of how much work had been done to get to this point, but then she paused.

Rationale

"What will we tell our employees when we tell them we're going to do this change?"

William Tenwirth piped in, "It doesn't matter whether they ask that question. We're doing this change because we're losing market share, and we cannot afford another quarter like the last one!"

"I'm not sure that's going to fly with the people in Customer Service," Torva interjected.

"What do you mean?" asked Dr. Alexander. William Tenwirth was frustrated with the response.

"Here's what I mean: Why did we consider this change? What are the long term company benefits of the change? And why are we doing the change at this time?"

"We don't need to answer those questions," William Tenwirth insisted, "I've done big changes like this before, and we just told people to get it done. Things went just fine." He was clearly exasperated.

"No, wait a minute," Dr. Alexander responded, "I think those are legitimate questions."

"I'm not concerned about that as much as I'm wondering about the make-up of the team," Andrea Beauchamp interjected, "my research group is going to want to understand who is involved and why".

"There are some other things you should consider," Luke Stinson added.

"Like what?" retorted William Tenwirth, growing more frustrated all the time.

"Well, what about the interfaces you have with other systems? And how different is the data from the two different companies? That can cost a lot more money in the long-run."

"Candidly, I'm confused about the impact of this thing," Tina Vasquez added, "What will this project affect in the short term? Long term? Who is affected by this?"

"Alright, I've heard enough questions for today. I thought you had worked these things out Jonathan," scolded Dr. Alexander.

"Well, we have a package and a few team members to get started," he answered sheepishly.

"Then we're clearly not ready for this change, are we?" Dr. Alexander asked, obviously concerned. "Today is Tuesday. By Friday, I want the questions that have been raised, answered, and this group will work together to get a comprehensive communications plan and scope determined. As far as I'm concerned, we're done for today."

The whole room got quiet as Dr. Alexander walked out without saying anything further, obviously frustrated with the situation.

*** FRIDAY ***

Due Diligence

The group convened on Friday. The tone was markedly different.

"Well, where are we today? Do we have a plan?" asked Dr. Alexander.

"Yes," Jonathan answered, "we do."   He turned on a projector and began his presentation.

"The rationale for this change is very straightforward: we have a global customer challenge that requires us to ensure we know where our products have been shipped and how our customers can access technical support from anywhere in the world."

He continued, "This project is expected to start on January 1st, and will start with a team comprised of IT and Sourcing."

"I'm feeling a bit more comfortable, but there is one gap that concerns me."

"What's that?" asked William Tenwirth.

"What about the systems that this new system will tie into? Who has checked that out?"

This time, William Tenwirth had something positive to say. "My financial team has done some very hard work the past few days and nights. We worked with IT to assess how things will fit together and we think we have a plan. We've added some additional funding in the event we missed some-thing critical."

Dr. Alexander nodded with cautious approval, "This is starting to come together," she thought to herself.

Intentional Communication

"There are two concerns that remains, at least at this point," she said to the team.

William Tenwirth shook his head in frustration. "We're ready to get this done, Miriam, what else could we possibly need?"

"As you recall, Torva asked a question at our first meeting about communication."

"Right," William responded tersely, "the whole customer service team—how they would respond."

"Yes, exactly."

"And they're not the only ones who need to know about this," Tina Vasquez chimed in, "Sales needs to know what's happening and when."

"Research, too," Andrea added.

William Tenwirth grudgingly admitted, "Finance will need to know, too."

Dr. Alexander pressed the issue further. "So, what about teams that aren't directly affected by this change? How will they find out what's happening?"

Tina Vasquez responded, "We whiteboarded all the groups that are affected by the project, and we will have a monthly get-together to explain our progress. We think we have them all."

"We need a complete communication plan for the duration of the project," said Dr. Alexander.

"That costs money," Tenwirth reacted.

"But, if people don't know what's happening, we'll spend more money," Torva responded.

Tenwirth wasn't pleased, but then he responded, "This is a big investment ... we need to make sure it pays off. Good communication is probably the right thing to do."

At that point, Dr. Alexander breathed an invisible sigh. "This is good progress, but I think we have a few more things to do before we launch the project."

Now Andrea Beauchamp was irritated. "With all due respect, Miriam, let's get on with this," she demanded, "We have a *lot* of customer complaints right now—we can't wait any longer."

"I understand Andrea, but Torva raised other questions that we cannot answer just yet, and I think it's critical that we've done our homework," Dr. Alexander said.

Andrea reacted, "What else could we possible need to know to get started?"

"Well, we need to find a way to have people let us know what's happening in the field," Dr. Alexander explained.

"What do you mean?"

"Well, what about the people in Johannesburg ? The former Brewster folks that are in the middle of the merger?" Dr. Alexander responded, "What happens when that team has trouble during the change?"

Andrea took a step back.

"And the team in Sao Paulo, what about them?"

"You're right; we need a way for them to let us know what's happening as the project gets rolled out," Andrea nodded in agreement.

Jonathan Smith reminded, "You said there were two things."

"Yes, I did," Dr. Alexander confirmed.

"So what else are you concerned about?" He asked.

Resistance

"What do we do with the naysayers? How will we manage them? I've been around skeptical researchers for a long time, and the naysayers can do some serious damage if we don't manage them," Dr. Alexander said.

Torva leaned forward, "You're right, some of them are truly skeptical, but they will come around. We need to work with those who have some significant influence in the corporation. How do we plan to do that?"

Dr. Alexander looked around the room, then asked, "Who are the most influential people in Catalyst?" It was an awkward moment. "Think of those people who have influence without high level titles; people who have been around a while; people who are well known—those are the people we want to work with."

"We can do that," Torva answered. Jonathan Smith nodded in agreement.

"So, where are we at?" William Tenwirth asked.

"Thank you for the question," Dr. Alexander responded. "By the next time we meet, I want a process or method for feedback, and a way to work with those who could challenge this project. Then we're ready to select a team leader and team to launch the change. And, we need some metrics to assess the effectiveness of the change along the way."

Metrics

"What?" Tina Vasquez asked, incredulous. "Metrics? What do you mean?"

"We need to measure the effectiveness of the change—it's that simple!" Dr. Alexander said, "We'll meet in a week."

They adjourned, again. Some in the group were visibly frustrated.

Tina Vasquez sighed to William Tenwirth, "I thought we were ready to go!"

"Yes, me too," Tenwirth grunted, "We need to get on with this ... why all the delay? It's driving me crazy."

"I like what she's doing," Torva interjected.

Tenwirth was not pleased with an underling offering input. "What do you mean, you like what she's doing?" he said, obviously irritated.

"She's using good Change Management practice, William," Torva explained.

"I'm not sure I understand," Tina admitted.

"She's preparing the organization for change the right way," Torva responded, "Her effort is going to go a long way in making the change successful."

William and Tina walked down the hall muttering about getting things done, but Torva smiled. She had done this before.

Launching the Change

* * * Monday * * *

Selection of Team Leadership

"Hope everyone had a good weekend," Dr. Alexander said, smiling at the group. "We have a lot to cover, so let's get to work. We need someone to lead this team from the beginning of the project to its completion."

As he heard this statement, Jonathan Smith was a bit puzzled, yet said nothing.

Dr. Alexander was perceptive. "I want to thank you, Jonathan, for all your help organizing and getting things started. It was necessary work, but clearly you have a lot on your plate right now, and this is going to get intense as we move into the next phase."

"You know, you're right", he said, nodding in agreement (and a bit relieved), "I do have a whole lot going on."

"We're going to need someone who clearly understands what we're trying to accomplish here, and someone who can communicate to our people, to our customers, to our partners. We also need someone who can keep the team on track."

Dr. Alexander looked around the room. Every leader in the room knew that the person who took on the project would be adding a significant amount of work to their daily activities. "Any suggestions?"

William Tenwirth spoke up: "Yes, I have a recommendation."

"Alright, what's your recommendation? Let's hear it." Dr. Alexander responded enthusiastically.

"Torva would be a great leader for this project. She understands what you're—we're—(he corrected himself) trying to accomplish here." His sincerity rang true.

Others nodded in agreement.

"Torva, what do you think?" asked Dr. Alexander.

"I would be honored, but I'll need some help."

Team Selection

"I agree," Dr. Alexander interjected, "We need everyone to pick up a piece of Torva's work, so she can focus. Who do we have for a team so far?"

Jonathan Smith took charge. "As I mentioned last week, we have good news for you, Dr. Alexander; we started to assemble a team of several people in the UK, with participation from IT, Sourcing, and Operations. We've chosen an off-the-shelf package from Navigator Software for logging technical support calls, and hired Luke Stinson from Navigator as the project leader. Navigator is headquartered in the US."

"I recall that discussion, but the representation seems a bit limited, don't you think?" wondered Dr. Alexander.

Torva confidently agreed, stepping quickly into her newfound role. "Dr. Alexander is right, we need people from Sao Paulo and Johannesburg, too, and we'll need several levels of management to account for the different challenges."

Jonathan Smith shot William Tenwirth a look of frustration, but Tenwirth did not reciprocate.

"We'll need members from all the Customer Service teams, Finance, and I'd like to know more about the people in the UK who can participate in the IT and Sourcing workstreams," Torva added. "And, I'll need a replacement managing the call center in Dallas."

"What about Natalie Simpson," Tenwirth asked, "I hired her a while back, and she seems very competent."

"If she'll take the role, she would be perfect for the job," Torva responded.

"What's a workstream?" Andrea asked.

"It's a team represented on the project plan," Torva responded.

Dr. Alexander liked what she was hearing.

Detailed Project Plan

"I'll need someone to own the project plan, too," Torva interjected. "I need someone who has all the details in a plan we can use to impact the change."

"Whoa, that's a lot of people!" William Tenwirth said loudly, "You're up to a team of nearly 15 so far."

"Yes, these teams tend to get a bit large, but this is a big investment, wouldn't you agree?" Torva asked.

"I thought you'd manage the plan," Tenwirth responded.

"No, I'll be very busy managing the communications with all levels, and ensuring that we don't run into any major snags," Torva explained.

"Who do we have to manage the project?" asked Dr. Alexander.

Risk of using the B team

"Well, I have a researcher who doesn't have a lot of work right now, and he might do a good job," Andrea Beauchamp responded.

"Will he maintain the plan and manage all the cost details? Time accounting? Manage vendor interfaces? Ensure we're all running on time? Does he have MS project experience? Has he worked in a high pressure team environment?" Torva asked.

Dr. Alexander looked over her glasses across the room at Andrea Beauchamp.

"He does not have that experience," Andrea admitted, "but maybe somewhere else on the project? It would be good to get him exposed to the wider organization."

"What's his skill set in research?" Torva asked.

"He is a great writer, extremely detailed and efficient," Andrea offered.

"We can use his skills managing the documentation from the IT systems, the process changes, and the technical training documentation," Torva responded.

At that point, Dr. Alexander felt confident that the group could move forward. "Anything else Torva?" she asked, obviously pleased with her new project leader.

"Yes, there are a few more things."

Tina Vasquez was visibly frustrated with the amount of effort going into the planning. "We just need to get this done—our customers are angry."

Team Cadence

Torva kept going. "How often will you want to meet as an executive team? I suggest every week, for starters. We will provide you with concise updates and give you a clear project status."

Feedback Loop to Assure Communication

"We'll also work with people in the field to provide a complete path for feedback because, in the event something goes wrong, we want to know about it immediately."

System Issues – Details for IT changes

Jonathan Smith interjected, "I think there are a significant number of IT issues we will need to address to ensure this goes well, including data transfer and assessing the disbanding of old systems at different sites. We discovered a lot of issues while we were taking an inventory of the systems."

Torva smiled, "Would you like to help?"

Jonathan Smith said, "Yes, if I'm not going to lead the project, I would like to be part of the team."

Dr. Alexander was pleased.

"Let's get this project done!" she said, enthusiastically. "We have officially launched!"

Supporting the Change

Operational Priorities competing with Change Project Priorities

After the meeting with Dr. Alexander, Tina Vasquez was energized to tell her sales team about the new system, but also wanted to know if the new product was ready and everything was on track. On Monday, Tina Vasquez typed an e-mail to Andrea Beauchamp, Chief Researcher:

"DuCharme Industries is rapidly gaining ground in Europe and America. We need the new product released *immediately*. When do you anticipate product launch?"

Later in the week, when Tina had not heard from Andrea, she walked down the hall to her office.

"Did you see my email?" she asked, walking into the office without knocking at the door.

"Yes, I saw your email," came the quick retort. "We are nearly ready to release the product, but several tests remain. We're working on it."

Tina pressed the issue further. "Are you confident we can outperform DuCharme's product?"

A bit irritated, Andrea did not look up from her computer.

Tina asked again, "Can we outperform DuCharme's product?"

Andrea looked over the top of her glasses, then responded. "These things take time. Products that heal human beings are complicated and complex. We don't turn them out like cardboard cutouts. You sales people are always rushing things. And besides, I have other activities going on with this new change project. My team is swamped."

"But six months ago you said it would be released by now. We have a major sales challenge. DuCharme is gaining serious market share and we need to have a big splash to show we're competitive. It's important that we meet the deadlines we set. We have customers waiting. We're not meeting our numbers!"

Visibly irritated, Andrea looked back at her screen. "I'll send you an email after I meet with the product team."

Tina walked away, muttering to herself. Later that afternoon, she received an email from Andrea Beauchamp:

"The product team says we will likely deliver first versions to the field in the next three weeks. It's a tight schedule, but I have been assured it can be done."

Armed with this new information, Tina arranged a conference call to inform her sales team that the new product was on it's way.

* * * Two months later * * *

DALLAS

Frontline employees and executive viewpoints

It was a normal day in Catalyst's Dallas Call Center– 500+ calls for orders, tech support and product returns.

Natalie Simpson returned from lunch to see twenty new emails in her inbox.

Two emails grabbed her immediate attention:

From: Tina Vasquez, Global Vice-President – Sales: LONDON.

NEW PRODUCT RELEASE - ANNOUNCEMENT

"I take pleasure in announcing that Catalyst will be releasing its new therapeutic web technology by September first. Watch for specific sales details. This product will provide significant advantage against our major competitor. Notify all managers and supervisors of the pending release. "

From: Luke Stinson, Project Leader – Navigator Software.

STANDARD GLOBAL CALL SHARING PLATFORM

"Greetings all North American call center team members. Within the next several weeks, Corporate will be releasing a new system for technical support calls. Watch for further updates! This system will be used globally in the coming months. I look forward to working with you."

Luke Stinson – Project Manager –   Navigator Software

Natalie Simpson read through both emails, and thought to herself, "Well, I'm glad they're going to release that new product—our customers have been screaming for it after the marketing campaigns—but I am concerned about this new technology for tech support. My team really needs to be trained. I do hope Corporate keeps us informed. My people will need time to learn the new system."

Managerial level versus organizational level

JOHANNESBERG

"This hiring process has been exhausting," Egan Mgebe said to himself, as he rubbed his eyes. "I never thought we would lose so many people when we were acquired by Catalyst."

Just before heading home for the evening, he quickly glanced at two new emails.

From Tina Vasquez, Global Vice-President – Sales: LONDON.

NEW PRODUCT RELEASE - ANNOUNCEMENT

"I take pleasure in announcing that Catalyst will be releasing its new 'therapeutic web technology' by September 1. Watch for specific sales details. This product will provide signifi-cant advantage against our major competitor.
Notify all managers and supervisors of the pending release. "

From Luke Stinson, Project Leader – Navigator Software.

STANDARD GLOBAL CALL SHARING PLATFORM

"Greetings all North American call center team members. Within the next several weeks we will be releasing a new

---

"Looks like the American call center has some changes
coming its way. I'm glad we don't need to be concerned about
a new system just yet–we have too many people to hire and
train on our existing system," he said, and shut off his
computer.

DALLAS
Incoming emergency calls from SAO PAULO

Surgeons at the Hospital Brigadeiro São Paulo SP
contacted the Dallas Help Desk. A traffic accident involving a
school bus on the Rodovia Adhemar de Barros caused multiple
injuries to 17 grade school children. The orthopedic surgeons
had decided to use Catalyst as their supplier for joint healing.

They discovered some technical challenges with the
methodology, and with such a large group of injuries, they
needed immediate assistance.

A phone call came into the Dallas Call Center from Sao
Paulo, requesting assistance on the new product.

Daniel Jackson, a customer service rep, sat at his desk,
staring at the computer screen. The new system came on line
that morning, and he was confused by what he saw.

"I'll never be able to do this—it's too hard; too complicated," he thought to himself.

Although he had been trained for several hours, the new
system was overwhelming.

"I'm going to look really stupid to these other reps; I can't even open a customer ticket."

Natalie Simpson walked by his desk.

"Everything okay Daniel?" she asked.

Daniel responded: "Things used to be a lot easier around here."

"What seems to be the trouble?" Natalie Simpson asked, a bit concerned.

The rep responded, "I cannot get this system to work, no matter how hard I try. I simply cannot access the data I need."

Natalie Simpson was professional, and hid her own concerns. She asked, "Did the training help?"

"Yes, somewhat, but it was a lot of detail packed into just a few hours. There is no way I can remember all the steps. This system is SO different from the one we used before. Everything is in the wrong place!"

"Well, do the best you can today. I'll get another rep to go over the training with you after your shift."

Natalie Simpson returned to her desk, frustrated and angry. "Does anyone know what's happening here? Those leaders in London completely missed the boat on this. They've failed and now we have to work it out."

She rapidly typed out an email to Luke Stinson, and copied Jonathan Smith.

From: Natalie Simpson, Customer Service   Manager – Dallas

STANDARD GLOBAL CALL SHARING PLATFORM

To: Luke Stinson, Project Leader - Navigator

Dear Luke, I'm not sure how you plan to manage the support we're receiving over here in Dallas, but my reps are very concerned about how the system works. Many of them cannot effectively respond to calls, and we have some severe emergency issues to deal with right now.

A reply came within minutes:

From: Luke Stinson, Project Leader – Navigator Software.

STANDARD GLOBAL CALL SHARING PLATFORM

To: Natalie Simpson

"Well, all your people were trained, and the system is operating the way it should. I don't understand your concern.
Luke Stinson – Project Manager –   Navigator Software

Natalie shot back another reply:

I don't think you understand. We are having trouble supporting customer orders!!!! I don't know what those people in London are doing.

Initiating the following response from Luke Stinson:

Well, it's really not my problem, I have other things to manage here. They were trained and, as leaders, you have to take charge of the change. The executive team is satisfied with what we've done. If you want, we have another training session for Europe happening at 3AM your time tomorrow. You could take advantage of that.

We liked the old way better versus the need to change.

The former Brewster employees in Johannesburg were alarmed and concerned. With all that was involved in the acquisition, they were buried in new paperwork, training and other organizational changes.

The call centre in Johannesburg buzzed like a hornet's nest with incoming calls for service. The new therapeutic technology from Catalyst had a major flaw, and hospitals across Africa were struggling with how to work with the new design. Surgeons wanted answers—now.

Egan Mgebe struggled to get his head above water through the barrage of phone calls. He was confused about the latest system changes, though he had been notified several weeks ago.

"I thought this would be a software patch like we did at the old company. I had no idea it would require a full system upgrade."

Egan heard the complaints of many of his reps.

"You're right," he said to his team, "In my old company, we wouldn't have had a system like this. Everything worked perfectly, and we didn't have ongoing problems. Those people in London have no idea what they're doing."

Egan pitched in to help with the technical issues, listening to calls and helping as much as he could. The team faced a few long days, working the weekend, finally getting through the challenge.

On Monday, Egan called the HQ in London. He was unable to reach Jonathan Smith, so he left a voicemail.

"Why did we implement this new system? It's terrible! All my reps can't stand it, either, and I agree with them. In my old company, we had much better tools. You people at Catalyst have no idea how to support and serve customers, and you have no idea what's going on out in the field. You're all going to destroy our customer relationships!"

A few hours later, Jonathan Smith sent an email.

Hello Egan – I received your voice mail. We are working around the clock to resolve the interface issues. You can check out our website for Frequently Asked Questions. We are updating them every day. Kind regards, Jonathan Smith

---

Egan angrily read the email and asked himself, "Why did we make this change?"

Finishing the Change

* * * Six Months Later * * *

Organizational Barriers to completion

Torva met Dr. Alexander in her office for a weekly update.

"Good morning Miriam, how are you today?"

"Doing well, thanks. The last team meeting went extremely well, don't you think?"

"Yes, it did, " Torva answered, "We're making significant progress. So how can I help you?"

"Well, frankly, we need to cut the size of your team. The people in Research and IT want their employees back, and I'm hearing complaints from several other departments that people are spending way too much time on the implementation of the new software."

Torva was a bit confused. "I think it's normal at this point. We have a lot of training going on, and we're not done with the managerial reports. There's still a lot of work to do. I need my team to stay intact."

"I understand your concerns, but certainly there must be a way. Research is getting pressure from me to add two new products.

CAUTION:
• Unforeseen Circumstances
• Leader mistakenly assumes the project is done
• Other priorities take the leader away from the project
• Boredom on the part of the leader

I'm convinced you can make it happen, Torva, and, candidly, it looks to me like the project is nearly done. I'm going to delegate the rest of the project to William Tenwirth. I want to thank you for your efforts, Torva, you've been a great leader."

Torva walked out of Dr. Alexander's office a bit shocked. On her way down the hall, she met Andrea Beauchamp.

"Hello Torva."

"Hello Andrea, how are you?"

"Doing well. Did Dr. Alexander tell you that we need to get our people back into Research? I hear the project is going well, and we need to get back to business."

"Yes, she did tell me. Thank you for their support," Torva said mechanically, but her mind was in another place.

When she returned to her office, she overheard several team members talking by the water cooler.

"I don't know how we're ever going to complete this thing. It just seems to go on and on," said one.

> **CAUTION:**
>
> - **Frustration—the 'grind' of the project**
> - **Distraction**

"I know. We had no idea it was going to take this long. I'm so over this project; I just want to get back to my real job."

"Yeah, I heard the new Research projects are incredible! I want to get on one of those teams!"

* * * One Week Later * * * *

Dr. Alexander walked into her office and flipped the switch on her computer, looking at some mail on her desk. She noticed a letter with her name handwritten on the front.

She opened it:

> *Dr. Alexander, I want to thank you for the opportunity to serve Catalyst. These past few years have been a great experience, and I have learned much. My last day will be two weeks from today.*
>
> *Warm regards,*
>
> *Torva Karachenko*
>
> *Cc: Denise Hamilton/HR*

Dr. Alexander frowned, then looked out the window. She thought to herself, "This project isn't finished. I need Torva's influence to complete it. I'm not sure how the team will respond when they hear this news."

She picked up her phone.

"Hello Torva," she said, relieved to get her on the line, "Do you have a few minutes for a cup of coffee?"

"Sure," Torva answered, "I'll meet you in the cafeteria in 15 minutes."

"That's great. See you soon."

They spent the next hour and a half talking through the project and Torva's concerns.

At one point, Torva said, "I'm not even sure if I'll have a job when this project is finished!"

Dr. Alexander made a request: "Could you hold off one day before announcing your departure from Catalyst? I have some phone calls to make and I'd like to talk with you again about your expectations."

Torva agreed to a one day delay provided Dr. Alexander would meet with the team one last time.

Architect's behavioral role in finishing the change

After her meeting with Torva, Dr. Alexander sat down at her computer:

To all Department Leaders:

While our Technology Introduction has made significant progress, we still have much to do. I recognize that I have asked for team members to step away from the project. We need to refocus our efforts the next few months to drive the project to completion. I will commit that your team members can return to you departments in three months. Between now and then, we need to put every bit of effort into finishing what we've started. I want a review of the status this coming Monday. We're all in this together – finger pointing solves nothing.

We started this project to better serve our customers and to improve our access to information for servicing our systems. Those reasons have not changed, and we need to finish what we started.

Miriam Alexander, CEO

Persistence

The following week Dr. Alexander met with the operations staff to check in on the change.

"How are things proceeding?" she asked.

Torva responded, "We have some serious challenges with the former Brewster team in Johannesburg. They need additional training and technical support. And the Dallas Center has some training needs as well. Overall, we need support when customers call in. It's still a challenge. "

Dr. Alexander continued "And the backroom technology operations? How are they proceeding, Jonathan?"

"We've had some slowdowns because we initially thought people were going to leave the project. Your email helped clarify the need to clean up the databases, and we now have a task force engaged in getting that done by the end of the month."

"So, clearly we are not finished with this technology introduction. What are the plans to support Dallas and Johannesburg?"

Torva and the rest of the team spent 90 minutes going through the details required to stay on task and complete the project. As they adjourned Dr. Alexander reminded them, "Next week; same time—let's keep this on track until it's done."

Clarity

Jonathan Smith stayed behind after the meeting for quick chat with Dr. Alexander.

"It's really getting tough to keep people on task, Miriam. People want to get off the project as soon as possible.

This isn't what they signed up for."

"As I recall, it was you who said, *'The rationale for this change is very straightforward: we have a global customer challenge that requires us to ensure we know where our products have been shipped and how customers can access technical support from anywhere in the world.'* That hasn't changed, *has it*?" Dr. Alexander asked.

"Well no, but people who have jobs in research want to get back to research," Jonathan insisted.

"I understand that, Jonathan, but let's face it: if we don't effectively compete with DuCharme, we may not have a research department to return to."

He tilted his head to the side, knowing she was right. The reason for the change had not changed.

"I'll spend a bit more time with them and explain the rationale again," Jonathan said. " ... strange that I had forgotten whey we started this in the first place."

Recognition

From Dr. Miriam Alexander to the   Technology Change Team:

Please join me in two weeks to celebrate the project milestones reached to date. I will be discussing the global successes of the project to date. Please ensure your local teams in Dallas and Johannesburg have refreshments and a comfortable place to meet. I want to talk about the achievements of several individuals who have worked through the challenges as we've all learned the new systems. There are several who have inspired us all!

One week later, Dr. Alexander asked for a conference call with key managers from both call centers and her entire leadership team. She explained what was happening at a high level, then asked for questions. Members of her executive team took note of the challenges field people were facing.

At the conclusion of the call, Dr. Alexander said, "We will send some training staff and technical people to work with you for a few weeks until we resolve these issues."

CAUTION:

- **Managerial Check-in**

- **Communicating to the end**

- **Renewing Vigor**

How will you know when you're finished?

* * * Eight months later * * *

The entire team gathered in the Boardroom at Catalyst. There were 35 people present. Dr. Alexander walked to the front of the room.

"Every change project is a new lesson for executives, and this has been no exception. I have learned much from everyone on this team, but a special thanks must be given to Torva Karachenko for her tireless efforts to ensure we spent our money, time and human talent wisely. Through her work with this project, Torva has been promoted to Vice-President of Customer Satisfaction. Please join me in congratulating her on this achievement!"

The team applauded.

"I've heard from many staff and leaders in Johannesburg, Atlanta, Dallas, and London that we have done it! We can now serve our customers in a truly global manner. We have some other information to share with you. Tina."

Tina Vasquez stood up. "We have not only stopped our loss of business, but within the past 2 months we have had significant success against our competitors. We are projecting a 14% increase in revenues and an 8% increase in profitability next year."

"Thank you Tina," Dr. Alexander continued, "I think we've learned much from this challenge and I am grateful for the hard work everyone put into this achievement. As a thank you, Catalyst will be adding 3% to each of your bonuses for the year. Thank you again!"

William Tenwirth stayed around until the end of the meeting and waited to talk with Dr. Alexander.

"You know, I had no faith that we could do this. None at all, really."

Dr. Alexander responded, "Yes, I was quite aware of that when we started this project.'

"Well ... I must confess," he said, with a rising sense of conviction, "Torva was right, you were right, and Catalyst's system is much better than Brewster's outdated customer logging software. This is really quite an achievement."

"Yes, it is," Dr. Alexander said, looking out her window, "Yes, it is."

Five principles for helping people adjust to Organizational Change.

Through decades of experience with team members across the globe, and by poring over hundreds of research articles, I have developed a few key principles for helping individuals adjust to organizational change. These five principles will give you specific areas to focus on as you help your organization adjust to new initiatives.

Let's start with this: leaders need to acknowledge human emotions.

Change Management Principle #1:

Reduce Anxiety to Increase Adaptation

While there are a few adventurous, novelty-seeking souls who enjoy constant change, the majority of people are wary of the 'new.' In business, the 'new' is often costly in terms of effort, time, money, and even physical discomfort (ever have to move your desk from one building to another?). Why all the fuss about things that seem so insignificant?

NEWS FLASH: The human brain is wired to conserve energy, and new things cause the brain to expend a great deal of energy. With energy expenditure comes anxiety, and with anxiety comes resistance.

SO!

Architects: Think about your people. What would REDUCE anxiety during change?

While there is no cookie cutter approach or cookbook here, I have some suggestions. Start by thinking about what would reduce team member anxiety. As a leader, what can you do to reduce apprehension and concern?

HINT: Lying doesn't help, nor do half-truths.

How does reduction in anxiety increase adaptation?

If my mind is *not* clouded by, say, whether I'll have a job when the change is done, or whether this change is going to completely upset the apple cart of my life, or if it is going to cause me to look incompetent, or if it will put me into a team with a bunch of people I have never worked with (or worse, with people I don't want to work with ...), my anxiety will be reduced. The reverse is also true. Keep me in the dark about the change and I promise to be ineffective during a time of great stress. The greater the unknown, the higher the anxiety, and the lower the adaptation.

Reduce anxiety, increase adaptation. If you want a change to 'take hold' in the DNA of your organization, this is not optional.

Real World Challenges:

MANAGING ANXIETY—PRACTICAL APPLICATION

I worked with two major pharmaceutical companies: one was careful to tell their team members about an upcoming change, and the other did not. At the risk of sounding cliché, one got the drug, and the other didn't. The company that did not provide clear messaging to their teams created a firestorm of employee dissatisfaction, resulting in what could only be described as a revolt. The other company had challenges, but they had developed significant trust through their ongoing communication, and completed a successful change.

Change Management Principle #2:

Simplify to increase adoption

I shall never forget a meeting I participated in as a sales executive, when I was promoted into a sales role. We were greeted by several, cheerful VPs on Monday morning around 8AM. They explained that we would be receiving 'training.' What followed is nothing short of amazing. From 8AM to 5 (sometimes 6) PM every day, we were subjected to a tag team line-up of the finest PowerPoint jockeys in the world, talking about every product, process and service we could sell.

At Friday night of that week, you could have looked me in the eye and asked, "what did you learn?" and, if I was honest, I would have said, "There's a lot of stuff to learn." I was exhausted, and probably not much smarter, but a whole lot wiser from the experience.

HINT: A key leader in the training world likes to say:

"TELLING AIN'T TRAINING."

I have witnessed (and I'm sure you have, too) events like the one I described. These events are developed by well-intended, efficiency-minded individuals ... who never sat through a session like that.

Learning Theory tells us something different: Distributed Practice is the key to retention.

What does that mean?

Research shows that smaller, intense bursts of training/ learning are superior to long, exhausting sessions that drain the mind, rather than fill it. "Massed practice" (the story about my sales experience) is the opposite (but the approach used quite often in corporations).

It means simplify to increase adoption.

Implications? When we're managing change, we need to provide people with enough knowledge to become competent,
without overwhelming them. In an age of online learning, Distributed Practice is eminently possible with any audience. In
fact, give them smaller bytes and they will love you for it.

What else do we need to do to simplify?

In any change, people can drown in a tidal wave of information. They will become fearful that they cannot absorb everything they need to know and, very often, they will become exhausted. Smaller, more compact and clear segments in
shorter bursts will help adoption rates. Change is not

easy. Complex change is hard. Offering people systematic
segments of carefully planned learning is a key element of
making the new change a part of your organization.

Simplify ... to increase ... adoption.

Change Management Principle #3 (from baseball):

Follow-Through to Assist Integration!

In tennis, golf, baseball, fly fishing, and just about any sport
requiring a fluid motion to achieve a goal, you hear the phrase
"follow-through." I love baseball, so I'll use that sport in my
analogy.

It's a simple thought, really. You have an intended action (hit
a homerun), you make a preparatory motion (pick up the bat),
you conduct a primary motion ("Swing batter, batter, batter"),
and then you follow-through. The only time a batter doesn't
follow-through is when they intentionally restrain the effort to
avoid a 'strike,' but no one hits a home run when they check
their swing.

Follow-through is just as important to the motion of swinging for the fences as any other part of the activity.

So! Why would we miss the follow-through in Change Management? Why check the swing?

Reasons managers must follow through:

Follow-through in Change Management is the most boring of the principles, but it is, in my mind, the most critical.

- People want to know if you're serious about this change. *Follow-through demonstrates commitment.*

- People have a lot on their plates, and it's easy to forget the new change. *Follow-through helps them to remember.*

- People sometimes resist change because it is costly. *Follow-through shows you are not changing the change. This change is going to happen.*

- People sometimes simply need reminders amidst distraction.

We all know the importance of 'sticking with something'

We've heard it from youth. Follow-through is nothing more (or less!) than persistence. We all know persistence pays.

If the change was worth investing in; if the change was worth the human effort; if the change will make a difference for your organization; if the change has long-term strategic value, then you need to follow through.

Change doesn't happen without follow-through. It won't become integrated into your organization if you don't persist. Follow-through to assist Integration!

Change Management Principle #4: Measure!

While we all have opinions about various and sundry things, in business, medicine, research, education and science, measurement trumps opinion. If you don't believe things can be measured, check the tax code—the government can measure anything!

Everyone has ideas, thoughts, concepts, and words we use to communicate what we're doing and, most of the time, we accept the progress we see from others, but when the time for change comes, we ***must*** measure.

In point of fact, we all have internal systems of measurement we use every day; for example:

"I think I've lost a few pounds."
"It seems like Jim has changed."
"Have you noticed how different the downtown area looks?"
"The manufacturer of those jeans seems to have cut back on quality."

We all evaluate things, ranging from the mundane to the critical. It's part of human nature to see how things transform, thus the need for measurement in change should not surprise us, but it often does.

Why measure?

For correction.

For celebration.

Correction When a change is underway, we need to take checkpoints along the way to assess whether the change is truly taking hold in our organizations. Clearly, with the heavy investments we make in change, a checkpoint is critical to assess whether we're truly making a difference in the fabric of our organizations, or if we simply appear to do so!

Celebration Teams work their hearts out when introducing new change. If you measure the impact of the change, you can demonstrate the value of their effort and reward them accordingly. Teams like recognition much better when they can see results (And so do executives!).

What reasons do people give NOT to measure?

1. It takes too much time.

2. We don't really have anything we can measure.

3. No one agrees on what to measure.

4. We don't have good data.

5. We don't have a simple system for measurement.

Now, think about each one of those excuses (because that's what they are) and ponder this: don't good managers measure performance? And, since they do, they have found ways to assess what's happening with people. Each of those excuses can be answered and resolved. Measure for correction and/or celebration. It's a great way to motivate people and navigate change.

Change Management Principle #5: Trust

We've reviewed four of my principles for effective Change Management. We come to the fifth and final principle: All change builds or destroys trust.

This principle sounds stern—perhaps even harsh—but, in my experience, it's true.

Think about it for a moment:

At different points in the history of your organizations, you've experienced changes that built confidence, and changes that eroded confidence, in leadership. You have felt a sense of leadership interest in the welfare of people and the interest of the organization, or you didn't sense it.

Though trust is a delicate thing, which is easily broken, it is also powerful element of influence in organizations.

If you sense that someone has your best interest in mind, and you see evidence of care and thoughtfulness, your trust increases; however, if you sense something is not right, your trust decreases.

Trust is a motivator like no other. When people trust their leaders during a time of change, they are inclined to add their personal energies to the task.

All change demonstrates the level of the organization's interest in the welfare of their employees, even in situations where the change may run counter to employee expectations.

Trust is built through...

1. Clear explanations of the rationale for the change

2. Constant and consistent communication of change progress

3. Training to help employees learn the new process or program

4. Support that helps people when they're challenged because of the change

5. Recognition of the extra effort people put in to make the change happen

6. Removing ineffective team members

Summary of the five points: *The five principles I have listed above are a great starting point for your further reading and discovery. What's important is that you take the time to:*

(1) *Accept the emotional nature of people – anxiety during change is a harsh reality*

(2) *Understand that people learn best in small bits*

(3) *Be very aware that follow-through is the path to accountability*

(4) *Remember that people like to see the progress of measurement*

(5) *People gain or lose trust with each new change*

Twelve Things to consider during an Information Technology Change

Technology changes are notorious for inducing major organizational trauma. Here are twelve specific areas where you must apply focus to achieve the ROI you seek when introducing new Technologies into your company.

1. Be careful of your own ROI Blindness

Perceived ROI sometimes makes rational people irrational. Rare is the organization that goes back to check the original ROI. Be brutally honest about the true financial and human toll required.

2. Take the time to assess your Organizational Preparedness for Change

The old gospel song asks, "Are you ready?" Have you thought through how this implementation will affect your organization? Do you have the capacity for this change? Have you conducted Organizational Diagnostics in the context of the IT change? Is the organization ready to work together to accomplish this change? Does the organization understand 'why?' Can the organization 'stay the course?' Are the leaders in place to manage the scope of the change? Have you conducted in-depth preparatory analyses to ensure a comprehensive understanding of all aspects of the IT scope?

3. Don't fall prey to using the "B" Team when only the "A" team will do

Are you fooling yourself into thinking that those with spare time on their hands are the right people for the job, simply be cause they are available? Think again.

4. Don't fall into the trap of denying the business impact of the change

Research shows your organization will not perform at the same level during the introduction of a new system. There are revenue and profit implications. What is your plan to address a revenue shortfall?

5. Grasp the fact that "The Wheels on the Bus go Round and Round."

Your organization needs to continue to serve customers and care for employees during the change. You are changing a tire on a moving vehicle–what are your contingency plans?

6. Beware of the Jimmy Hoffa Syndrome

Your system project will cause you to discover unexpected software patches that must be integrated with the new system, some built in COBOL (= $$$$). Uncover those pitfalls early in your due diligence!

7. Think hard about the song "I get by with a little help from my friends."

Your implementation is going to impact a LOT of unforeseen individuals and teams. Discover who will be impacted. I can assure you, the impact matters to them, and if you don't prepare them for the impact, you will have slowdowns costing millions!

8. Be alert to the "Ado Annie" Syndrome ("I can't say 'No'").

Ado Annie was a character from the famous Broadway musical "Oklahoma!" and famous for the phrase, "*I can't say no.*" Without discipline, projects grow into monstrosities, becoming impossible to implement. Scope happens. Manage scope or it will manage you. Say no.

9. Do not allow your team to write Technology Code before conducting full blown process analysis.

Do not write Technical Design Documents without first having gone through Process Design. Resist this impulse or you'll automate a bad process.

10. Make sure you "count the cost."

The Biblical adage about ensuring you can finish what you start is wonderful, ancient wisdom. Consider the whole cost in people, process, finances, time, and effort. Are you determined to complete the project?

11. Don't ignore the details; this is painstaking work, but worth the time and effort.

1. *Agree on the meaning of terms—make sure there is no ambiguity on what something means. This is crucial on global projects.*

2. *Develop standard definitions of terms.*

3. *Design consistent revision controls and stick to them.*

4. *Ensure consistent issue management.*

5. *Construct common databases for efficiency.*

6. *Develop agreed upon disciplines*

7. *Ensure project controls from the start*

8. *Ensure revision controls*

9. *Issue controls*

10. *Map processes before automating processes*

12. Be careful not to develop an adversarial relationship with your vendors.

Developing an adversarial relationship leads to unnecessary stress and multiple excessive challenges you can avoid by up-front clarity and ongoing dialogue.

HERE'S HOW YOU <u>KNOW</u> YOUR ORGANIZATION IS READY TO DEPLOY A MAJOR INFORMATION TECHNOLOGY CHANGE

Organizational Readiness for Change:

○

The Organization is ready for change when...

- They are emotionally and technically prepared for the change

- They are prepared to execute all customer interactions

- They have a management organization (up to, and including, executive levels) that can effectively manage the business

- They have data viability for all affected systems

- They are able to conduct necessary financial reviews

- They have post-deployment support established

- They have enough support staff to answer questions the day the question is asked, and

- The have validated interoperability with other teams (systems, equipment, factory, people).

Figure 9 – Organizational Readiness for Change

The Priceless Value of Leadership Humor

When I am asked about qualities I value in someone leading change, people are often surprised to hear me say, "A leader needs a great sense of humor."

Why would a sense of humor be a key trait in a good leader?

1. People are under radical stress in the workplace.

2. People work incredibly long hours.

3. People give their lives in support of a job.

4. People lose precious family time in support of the workplace.

5. People's lives **outside the workplace** are often complicated, adding to the stress (Work-Life Balance anyone?).

Objections to leadership humor:

1. Humor can be perceived as disrespect, lewdness, and crass behavior, possibly leading to harassment charges.

2. Humor diminishes the seriousness and gravity of the work. Leaders need to be dour, grim and stern. "Stiff upper lip," and all that sort of thing.

3. Humor demeans a leader and turns him or her into a class clown, causing a loss of respect from employees.

4. Humor can be misperceived in a global environment.

I take each objection in turn ...

1. Lewd behavior and humor has no place at work (or anywhere else, but that's my personal bias in favor of respect for others). Clearly, any humor that harms another individual or causes someone to be uncomfortable is out of place, but that's not the kind of humor I'm talking about; I'm talking about having a bit of fun in the midst of stress.

2. When the situation requires gravity, the leader knows it, and the people know it. They all sense the need for seriousness, but a constant pressure of seriousness creates emotional distress for employees, adding even MORE stress to their work. People need to laugh now and then—"comic relief" is valuable in the workplace.

3. If a leader is CONSTANTLY cutting up, he or she will lose the respect of the people; but, an intelligent quip at the right time not only adds to a leader's persona, it makes him or her—ready?—"human!" With the exception of warfare, I can't imagine a place where the occasional quip is out of place. A leader who can tell a joke (and, even better, *take* a joke!) will create an emotional bond that is hard to break under pressure.

4. In a global environment, things don't often translate well ... but ... if you explain a joke or concept, people across the world love to laugh! One of my greatest communication victories ever was to tell a joke cross culturally with a group of Japanese business people, who laughed very heartily at the punch line ... when explained through an interpreter.

Summary: Leadership humor is free, but it is also priceless *Effective humor endears people to a leader, because laughter is good for the soul; it eases pain, refreshes, and adds energy when needed. Never underestimate the motivational power of leadership humor—it demonstrates a* *quick mind, intelligence, emotional sensitivity and, most of all, develops a bond of human contact unattainable by any other means. A little laughter goes a long way.*

Dr. Jim Bohn

Serving in a variety of roles in the corporate world since 1973, Dr. Jim Bohn has personally lead the transformation of multiple, underperforming teams to achieve award-winning levels of success.

After several decades with a Fortune 100 Company, Dr. Bohn launched a Change Management and Organizational Transformation Practice called ProAxios.

Dr. Bohn has personally led significant Change Management projects, including IT implementations, mergers, and reorganizations, in roles ranging from the shop floor to design, and from engineering to sales and service, along with global experience in change and operations.

Dr. Bohn taught Organization Development at the University of Wisconsin's LUBAR School of Business, Business Ethics and Strategy at Concordia University, and Leadership at Marquette University. Deeply passionate about learning, developing, and practicing organizational research in the context of change, Dr. Bohn is a Master Facilitator and has led hundreds of workshops with audiences ranging from frontline mechanics to Senior Vice-Presidents in the Fortune 100.

To learn more about Dr. Bohn, go to: http://proaxios.com/

Twitter: @DrJimBohn